"THEY"

WHAT DO THEY WANT?

DAVE EMMONS

HANGAR 1 PUBLISHING

CONTENTS

1

FIRST UFO SIGHTING

My UFO/ET experiences have been happening, it seems, for a lifetime. As you read through this book, your first thoughts will likely be how did one person experience all these highly strange events? I often wonder that as well. Why did extraterrestrials take an interest in me? Throughout this book, I will refer to some of my family history, especially my mother. One popular theory is that extraterrestrials follow family DNA frequency lines. I have offered to people in the past that I would submit to a lie detector test (polygraph) to support my honesty of what I am about to disclose to the world.

These incredible, otherworldly experiences started when I was 13 years old. My first encounter was in 1962 in the backyard of my house in Alton, Illinois. Even now, in my regressed memory, I remember this UFO event very clearly. It was a lovely summer evening around 8:30 pm, just starting to get dark. I did not want to go in the house, it was too hot inside, we had no air conditioning and I was not done playing in the yard. In my wildest imagination, I could not imagine what was going to happen next. I remember standing up and looking to the western sky. As I looked toward the horizon, I saw this strange craft about 100 feet in altitude slowly floating over my house. Of course, being a kid, I could not make accurate size estimations. My best guess was that this UFO was 40 feet wide and was a rectangular-shaped craft. I remembered looking at the light blue pulsing lights at the bottom of the UFO. Being a youngster, I was afraid of what this craft would do.

CHAPTER ONE UFO 1962

(Author note: After seeing the strange craft, I felt inside me an expectation to see these visitors, as if someone had planted this thought in my head. As time went on, I would recognize these expectations for future events—a telepathic messaging that I would become quite familiar with.)

The craft looked like a small barge due to its flat shape. There were four bright white lights on the leading edge of the UFO and it appeared to be a dark metallic gray color but this could have been affected by the darkness of the evening. I was scared for a minute upon first seeing this craft, likely because of the scary Martian movies I had seen recently. This fear did not last long during this short conscious state of observing the craft. Were the aliens coming to get me for food and take me away? My mother would not have been alarmed about my missing because she thought I was at my friend's house. After the short observation, I cannot remember anything that followed.

My mind went blank staring at the craft, and I had no recollection of time. My memory did not start working again until I found myself in my shared bed with brother Jack. I don't remember how I got back in my bed. I awoke in a panic, not knowing what had just happened. I felt a presence next to me by the bed just after I woke up but could not make out who or what it was. I reached to touch my right leg because I could not feel anything; I was numb. Later I would refer to numbness as dumbed down, not being able to control my thoughts or movements. I tried to speak out to my brother, but no words would come out. The object or entity next to my bed disappeared and I felt safer. I was exhausted, and felt that probably gave reason to my falling asleep quickly. I woke up my brother.

"Did you see or hear anything last night?" I asked him.

"No, why?" He responded.

I launched into telling him about the UFO event, and of course, he just laughed. Extraterrestrials (ETs) are known to put everybody else asleep and pick their target person to work on.

After this UFO incident, I became more aware of my surroundings and kept my eyes on the sky more when I was outside. I would try to keep my other siblings around me while we played in the yard. Consciousness? It looks like I learned that trait early on in life. As a young boy trying to tell this story to my family and friends was an uphill battle. Years later, my family would learn about UFOs and join me in sharing strange stories.

A question that I was also left with was why this craft flew over my family's house. As you read on, you will hear of a second saucer craft hovering over my backyard. Years later, my brother Jack asked me, "how are you so sure you were the only one taken by this saucer in the family that night?" I would be a wise man if I could figure out why ET abduct certain people. Your soul's consciousness and energy matrix are taken in some abductions, not your physical body. Yes, I said matrix and an Avatar version of yourself is abducted. Fifty percent of people abducted don't even have any memory of the event (Dr. David Jacobs). Little did I know, I would experience multiple times after the incident in 1962.

2

SECOND UFO ENCOUNTER WITH A FRIEND

Less than a year after my UFO encounter, my best friend Dave and I witnessed a close-up UFO sighting. It was the beginning of summer in 1963, and we had just finished the school year. At around 10 pm, and my friend and I were enjoying the music from a ten-transistor radio, drinking Pepsi Soda from glass bottles sitting on his steps to his basement apartment. We were having one of those young boys talk sessions about school and going fishing while enjoying a lovely quiet evening and nice weather: just a few small rain clouds but no rain. As we sat there, something life-shaping happened to both of us.

First, we noticed the ten-transistor radio cracking and popping.

"Did you change the batteries?" I asked.

"Yes, I did just a while ago." He answered.

The second sign of something happening was the smell coming from the sky. A strong sulfur-like smell or that of hot electrical appliance odor drifted through the air. Both of us stood up and started looking around. Above the treetops appeared eerie white lights just floating above the trees.

"Hurry up, let's go to dad's truck for a flashlight." Dave jumped up, heading in the direction of the truck.

"Do you think we can communicate with it?" I asked him.

He nodded, "Yes, let's go."

We ran up to the street level where his dad's truck was parked. Dave got the flashlight from the truck and pointed it at the low-flying saucer. He quickly started turning it off and on. The craft seemed to notice the flashlight blinking, and it, too, blinked its lights back at us. Both of us were amazed by what we were seeing. I slightly understood what this strange craft was, considering the Deja Vu I had experienced in the backyard last year. We walked up the street slowly, never taking our eyes off this craft. We never called it a UFO because back then, we didn't use this term. From the movie terminology we learned, it was a flying saucer. Rapid conversation went between us about what we were seeing, making sure we were on the same page. Our parents had told us never to approach a flying saucer, but we went straight at it, ending up in an empty lot just behind my backyard.

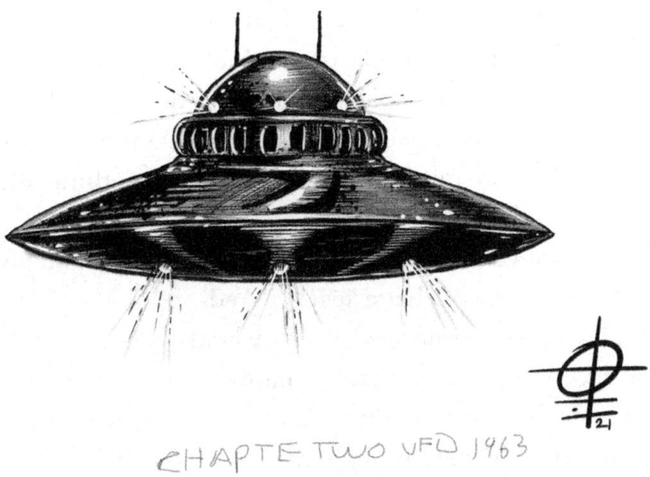

We had to verify what was going on with every step we took as we walked up the road.

"Do you see what I see?"

"Can you believe we're seeing this?"

Then the saucer stopped moving, about 75 feet above my backyard. The funniest part about this adventure was before we lost track of time, we pinched each other to make sure we were awake and not dreaming. Dave pinched me hard.

"That hurts, Dave." I yelped.

"At least you are awake like I am." He shrugged, grinning.

The craft did not belong to our military. It made no sound, did not have a visible means of propulsion, and moved too low and slow for the existing technology in 1963. Dave turned off the flashlight.

"We don't need this anymore." He stated. This was the final moment. We just stared in awe at what we were seeing.

Dave asked me again, "do you see what I am seeing?"

"Yes, I do, but I am afraid to look at them if they come to the portals around the craft."

It was at that time we stopped talking around 10:30 pm. We had no watches, so we could not tell the real-time, just guessing.

The saucer was about 75 feet high and 100 feet away from our position. There were no people other than us outside that night. Most of the neighbors were in bed, including our families. There was no streetlights shining over this empty lot. No trees were blocking our view of the craft, giving us excellent visibility. From what we could tell, it was a thick round saucer that looked like an old-time toy top that you wound up with a screw handle. It could have been mistaken for the WWII saucer the Nazi's experimented with. The craft appeared to be 50 feet wide and 25 feet tall. It had three rings on it like the toy top. The color was a dark gray metallic with no seams or bolts. There were no markings or symbols on the craft either. The bottom was dark black from burning into our atmosphere. The first section was about 10 feet thick; the second section was about 10 feet thick, where the portals (windows) were located. There were portals all around the craft, and it seemed they could have been one-way viewing windows. Portals were 3 feet by 3 feet estimated. My concentration was on the portals because I feared seeing the ETs. Remembered, that was the last thing I said to my friend, "I didn't want to see these aliens." Dave saw shadows and pointed them out to me. On the top level of the saucer was a five-foot-tall hatch-looking piece with two antennae on top. Also, a small red light off to the side on that top section.

"I heard a buzzing sound from the saucer." Dave said. We both spoke a little more, but I did not remember what we said until my regression years later.

After that last moment of talking about the buzzing sound, neither one of us remember anything. We just ended up where we were standing when we first saw the saucer. Even now, I can place the saucer taking off very fast to the west of my house through the clouds. When we initially saw the saucer, the craft was to the southwest of my house. I don't remember Dave mentioning the craft's take-off direction. At this time, we were both excited and shocked by what we saw. We just needed to go home. The last thing we said to each other was we would tell our family about this sighting.

As soon as we both came to consciousness after the sighting and just before we took off for home, we seemed to be kind of numb, and totally out of focus for a couple of minutes. This was a clear sign of being abducted and memory erased by the ETs. Due to my previous event almost a year ago, I knew about having memory erased with body numbness subconsciously.

But, when I got home, my mother had to unlock the door for me.

"Do you know what time it is?" She asked, irritated.

"But I saw a flying saucer mom." I responded excitedly.

"I will flying saucer your butt, now get to bed."

During this time, she kept her flying saucer experience away from us kids because of the big scare during those years, and she did not want to scare us more. Dave went home and told his dad, and his dad simply said, "Yes, son, now get to bed."

My gut feeling was that we had an hour or so of lost time during the sighting. People laughed at us when we told our stories. Even our classmates gave us a hard time with our experience.

Following this UFO event in 1963, I found a mysterious lump in my testicular area a couple of weeks later. This object was in my left testicle area. There was an inch long, thin red line on top of the weird lump as though I had been cut by a laser. The lump bothered me because I did not know what it was and so, I decided to try and remove the lump through the red line. I assumed (correctly) that this red line was cut in order to insert whatever the lump was into my testicular area. Though I was only 14 years old, I knew that the visitors purposely did this operation. I pushed the object out of my testicle area. It hurt just a little, but there was no blood around the red line. It's almost like it was meant to come back through the red line.

When I got the object out of the testicle, it was hard, about 5/16" long and ¼" thick, was an ash light tan color. While holding the object, it started to turn a darker brown due to the air changing its color. I brought it to my mother and showed it to her.

"What is it?" She asked.

"I pulled it out of my testicle area." I responded.

"Throw that thing away. It is just ingrown hair."

"No, Mom. I pushed it out where there was red line. There was no blood or much pain while pushing it out." My mom went quiet in deep thought about this object.

"Throw it out anyway." She said finally.

I saw confusion in my mom's replies about this object. She connected the dots between my saucer story and the strange implant. Her quietness, intentional, because she did not want to scare me more than I already was. During the sixties, the average person did not know about implants or erased memories from abductions. People thought that when a person got abducted, they were never coming back. And most people thought ETs were using us as food and we would disappear. People paid more attention to Martian movies than the actual science. Our scientists were not speaking about this phenomena during those years, as our government would not allow scientists or academia to discuss flying saucers.

After the encounter with the UFO, I felt that what the ETs were interested in from me was how I learned how to talk and read. I would have random, flashbulb memories of different things. Pictures of the "Tom and Jerry" kids' readers, especially the back cover with a giant horseshoe with animals all around it. The movie "Five Gates to Hell" popped up, too. The movie star Vera Miles also surfaced as the ETs extracted memories from me so they could learn how to be human. ETs often tap into our subconscious to understand our emotions.

The 1963 UFO event was regressed in lucid dreams later in life. I did not know when this dream occurred, but lucid dreams are too realistic to forget. I dreamt I was on a shiny metal table in a dark room dazed, sleepy condition. It was warm in this room, and the air felt stuffy, hard to breathe. I did not notice my friend in this room with me. Somebody or some entity was helping me put my shirt back on, but the shirt was too small for me because it was my friend's. So, I figured he was there onboard the UFO, I just did not see or hear him. While we were still dumbed down, the ETs dressed us and put us back where we were in the empty lot, standing right where we got picked up.

I saw the UFO speed away from our position, going straight up west. I was never sure my friend saw the UFO leave, and he does not remember being abducted, but even now, we talk about this UFO event almost every time we get together. The missing time, abduction, and direction of UFO leaving were still unanswered until this regressed lucid dream gave me some answers. The dream also let me know that the UFO moved about 30 degrees without us knowing it to the west from the southwest. I drew this UFO movement scenario out on paper when I went back years later to look at the location. The drawing confirmed movement of UFO without us seeing it move and what that means is we were abducted. To quoting Dr. David Jacobs, "If you are within a hundred fifty feet of a UFO, you are their target."

I reflected on the implant in my left testicle after some years passed and believe that it was designed to go into my bloodstream and change and enhance my DNA. I believe that later in life they took semen samples from me several times. The implant would have dissolved into my DNA, but I am not sure the results the ETs wanted. But as I said earlier, those implants are not for locating us like a GPS beacon, their purpose is much larger.

3

UFO GLIDER THIRD ENCOUNTER

The next close up experience I had was in 2001. It had been years since I had seen a close-up view of a UFO. During these empty years of not having ET experiences, other than things like orbs moving in the sky, I never saw anything identifiable that I was excited about after having seen two very close-up UFOs in the past.

At the time, I worked as a Vacation Breaker (leadman) in a Gasoline Cat Cracker Unit. I regularly checked the vessels, motors, and product lines. One evening, I was up on a Reactor vessel at 140 feet of stairs, standing on a deck around 11 AM when I saw something bright and shiny coming towards me from the east of the Refinery. It looked as though it was 20 more feet higher than my position as it drew near me. What struck me as strange was the low speed at which it was traveling. It was illegal to fly over a Refinery with an aircraft, so I called the Control Room and told the guys what I was seeing. They laughed and said, "that is alright, we will pass on this one." As I watched this glider-looking craft, I noticed it had no cockpit, no pilot, no means of propulsion, and was smooth as glass. It had no bolts or metal seams. It was very quiet.

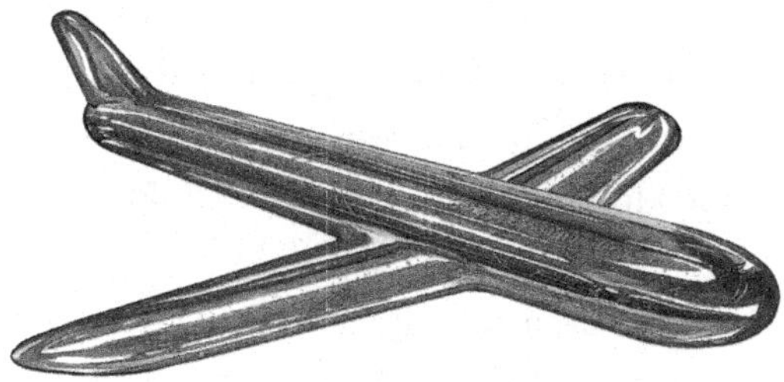

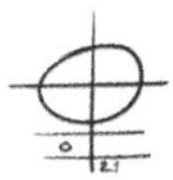

As I stood watching this UFO craft, I judged it to be about 20 feet long and 16 feet at the wingtips. The fuselage was four feet in diameter. It had two typical wings and one vertical tail wing. The longer I watched it, the more I felt some energy coming off the UFO. As it glistened in the sun, it came within about 40 feet of me. I watched it for five minutes, then it headed south slowly and out of my sight. I felt a tingling sensation all over my body as it passed by me. This was not a military or commercial glider, there were just too many odd technical differences. The five minutes of contact with the craft seemed to communicate telepathically with me. The UFO was uploading from me and downloaded some information that would avail itself in a couple of nights. An ET drone? I figured it had to be because you would have to be small to pilot something that size.

A couple of nights later, I had a very lucid dream about the craft over the Refinery. At the time, our company was in the process of remodeling our gas plant and had spent 6 million dollars on the renovation. My lucid dream placed me in my unit of operation. It felt as if I was there in a physical form. All my lucid regressed dreams have been interactive and felt genuine. As I walked around the machinery in this dream, I did not hear a sound. Usually, the plant is loud, and you need earplugs for safety. When I got to the massive blower room motor, it, too, was silent. I became alarmed that the unit was down. I ran into the control room, but it was dark, no operational lights were on, nobody was in the room. It was empty. As I was standing in the middle of the room, something told me subconsciously that our plant was closing soon. This message likely had come from the download of the glider UFO I encountered a couple of days ago.

After I had the lucid dream of the gas plant closing, I became sure it was correct; I told my workmates the next day what I thought. They argued with me because of the 6 million dollars being spent on the plant for renovations.

"Why would the Company close the plant? You are crazy, Dave," they all said.

I told them I would make a bet with them. The lucid dreams that I have are very factual and always come true. I told them in four months, the plant would close. After that conversation, I was out of work for several months following a back surgery. During my time off, in precisely four months, the plant closed. The lesson here is, don't ever ignore an absolute lucid dream because there are facts built in the dream.

A lot of knowledgeable people have had dreams and possible downloads for knowledge. Some geniuses like Tesla, Einstein, and Warner Von Braun attributed their spark of wisdom to life forms in the universe. They pointed to the sky when asked where they got their ideas. My story contains tiny bits of information, not wisdom. I could only wish.

ETs downloading future events only prove they know time travel and control time. Coming within proximity to ETs either slows time down or speeds it up. Most people I have interviewed say time stood still, or it was so fast their minds were unable to keep up.

4

FOURTH UFO ENCOUNTER

I55 PIE CUT UFO

This UFO sighting started with a Lucid dream. In August of 2010, I had a vision of being in a small nightclub watching a band setting up equipment on an oval-shaped stage. The female singer, who I knew, was at the bar. Her husband was the drummer in the band. She got up to go to the restroom as I spoke to her husband. As I was speaking with him, I saw a very tall, darkly dressed figure standing in the corner of the stage. This entity was at least nine feet tall. It seemed like I was in an old Rome setting, with urinals out in the open, but I was in Springfield, Illinois, in the downtown center.

A month after I had the vision about the nightclub, something told me to go out that night and listen to my friend's band. I was tired and did not feel like going. This urge to go to the nightclub in Springfield got stronger even though I felt exhausted. I remembered the last time I felt tired; something told me I was supposed to go. I would witness something if I went where they told me to go.

At about 7 PM that evening, I went to Club Marley in Springfield, Illinois. I got there at 8:45 PM and met my two musician friends. I saw exactly what I saw in the vision a month earlier as I entered the bar. The stage was a half-moon shape, and musicians were setting up musical equipment. I sat at the bar with my friend "J" and drank with her. I told her about being in this club before in my dream. She was a singer and a psychic and knew about strange energies. We knew each other from the UFO Group we had in Springfield. As I told her about the vision, I told her she should take pictures of the dark corner of the stage. In the corner of my eye, I could see a tall, dark figure standing there. She told me she had goosebumps hearing this story. She got up to go somewhere in the club and I asked her if she was going to the bathroom. She said yes, and I told her I saw this also in the vision. "J" mentioned that this is weird. I told her about the old Roman outside urinals on the stage area. Since we are both empaths, it seemed magnetic energy started surrounding us. After an hour and a half of hearing my friends play music, I left, feeling it was time to go.

When I got to my car in the back lot, I saw this young lady reaching across her car console, staring at me. This had to be around 10:45 PM. She was going for something, it seemed. An eerie feeling accompanied the way she stared at me while I was pulling out of the parking lot. Brushing it off, I got on the road out of town. There are a lot of stoplights on this road and it seemed I was speeding, going through them. I kept checking speed, and I was just fine with the speed limit. But I was in one of those partially dumbed-down modes like I was not focused mentally. It took me less than 10 minutes to get out of town through all these stoplights and arrive at the McDonald's at the south end of town. My friends told me that it takes a lot longer than 10 minutes to get through all those stoplights. I stopped at McDonald's, where I got a drink and used the bathroom.

After I got on I-55 south to head for home in Godfrey. I figured it would take one hour and a half to get home from that point. I drove about four miles south on I-55 and saw a bright light coming up the highway from the south to the north. This light was near the northbound lanes about a mile away from me heading south. At first, I thought it was a helicopter monitoring traffic. As I got closer, I noticed it looked strange. I slowed down from 60 MPH to 40 MPH to look at this object with a bright light coming my way. The thing got within a quarter-mile of me on my left. I rolled my window down to get a closer look. Several cars and vans were traveling with me in a group scattered out on the highway. I knew the object looked strange by the motion and low-level altitude at which it had when approaching me. I slowed down to 25 MPH and stuck my head out of my driver's window. I saw the UFO go over the top of my car, barely missing the powerlines on the other side of the highway. It crossed directly over my car, and with all the other vehicles on the road, that was strange; why my car?

The UFO was traveling around 30 MPH and 25 feet directlyabove my car. I could only see the bottom of the craft, and it was exciting to see another one so close up. It was about 40 feet wide and somewhat thinner than other craft I have seen. I could not make out the top of the UFO due to being under it. The bottom looked like a pie cut into four slices parted by dark lines. In the center, the UFO had a dark circle about 10 feet in diameter. The panels (pie cuts) were glass-looking material that emitted all the light. The UFO accelerated after it passed over my car and disappeared west of the highway. There was no sound and no means of propulsion except for the bottom lights.

Why did the UFO craft fly directly over my car when several other vehicles on the highway were close to me? Again, I felt slightly disoriented and dizzy during that closeness with the UFO. Magnetic energy filled up my car because I felt a familiar weakness after it passed me. Time felt like it was speeding up; my car's speed remained within limits. It was 55 MPH. Since my mind was foggy, I kept an eye on my car's speed. During that time, my drink spilled on my shirt. After another exciting UFO encounter, I was highly energized.

I had found out what the vision from the nightclub was about. It was to position me for a UFO encounter. Telepathically, but ever so subtle in its delivery. The lights seemed to blur, and I was in a tunnel driving down the highway as if through a time jump. A conscious connection that created synchronicity of events communicated by ET. And who was the young blonde lady reaching for her console and maintaining a stare in the parking lot?

When I drove down the driveway to my house in Godfrey, it was 11:30 PM. It had taken me 40 minutes less than any other time I had made that trip from Springfield. The ETs can speed up time, slow down time, and see into the future. Could ETs be time travelers that check in on us humans from time to time? Or are they us in our future? That would mean they can go back in time, countering scientists who have difficulty theorizing that possibility. I see a pattern in abductions. ETs first telepathically communicate to you to be somewhere, making you tired with magnetic energy. Next, they abduct a person and do medical procedures like removing eggs, collecting semen, and taking DNA samples. Though there have been cases where people were dropped off at different places where ETs began the abduction process, they usually return you to the last location you were at before this process started.

5

BRIGHT TUBULAR SHAPED UFO

The same synchronizing encounter with a UFO happened again on January 2, 2011. That evening, I got another telepathic message to go see the movie "The Tourist". I did not want to see that movie because I did not think it was going to be enjoyable and the ratings were low. On the way to the film, while driving on I-255 east, my trunk lid opened on its own. It was 6:55 PM when I got out of the car to close the trunk. At the same time, a small craft (a UFO) flew over me and did not make a sound. This craft was about 200 feet above me as it passed by. The location was near the SIU Campus, Edwardsville. Though I saw this bright shiny UFO orb but could not make out the craft's structure. The craft stopped about a half-mile south of my location. It remained stopped until I got back in my car. It felt like it was purposely watching me – a strange feeling. Then the orb left, and I did not see it again.

After watching the boring movie, I started back on I-255 north to my home. I stopped to pick up some store items and proceeded north again. When I got to Fosterburg road, I looked to my left or west of the I-255 to the tree line area. There I saw a very bright tubular UFO illuminating the darkness. It was about 60 feet long with a smaller white orb in front of it. I could not discern any other features of the UFO. I guess you would call this a modern-day military tic tac appearing UFO. This craft paralleled my car and kept pace with my speed of about 60 MPH. This took place around 10:28 pm.

This UFO tic tac seemed to disappear, but it must have been hovering over my car because I felt the energy. I started feeling weak and a hot, flushed feeling. I pulled off to the side of the highway because I was afraid of driving due to being vulnerable and disoriented. Yes, I knew this feeling; I was being hit with magnetic energy. Like I was drunk, I got chills, dizzy, and both eardrums were popping. I stopped the car and waited until I felt like my usual self. It felt like ETs were uploading my memory. I did not know precisely what had happened to me on the side of the road. The energy was real, and my body symptoms were a natural reaction to the same feeling that I have felt in the past. Luckily, no cops were around to check me out during this weakened state.

I must have been on the emergency ramp of the highway for at least five minutes. This was an unusual time and place to manipulate my brain functions for uploads, but ETs often show up at the most unlikely of times and places. When I got home, I felt energized to the point of not being able to sleep.

6

LARGE TRIANGLE UFO

My sixth up close UFO sighting happened on April 9, 2011, around 8:30 pm, just a couple of hours after arriving home from the Ozark UFO Convention in Eureka Springs, Arkansas. The weather was cloudy, as if it was going to rain. I was in my driveway talking to my brother Mick on a landline phone when I saw a couple of large bright white lights approaching me about a half-mile away from the north. The lights seemed to be very low to the ground. I told my brother I would call him back and that I had seen something strange.

I stood watching these two lights coming directly at me. I thought that these lights were very strange and I stood mesmerized and once again, I felt Déjà Vu all over with another UFO sighting. As the craft approached me, I could finally make out the shape of the craft. It was a large Triangle UFO about 40 feet off the ground and traveling 30 MPH. As the Triangle craft began to pass over me, it brushed the top of my neighbor's tree on the other side of my street in Godfrey, Illinois. The center of the Triangle was right over me, and I could make out the bottom of the UFO's structure. The size of this craft was shocking. It covered my whole street, about nine houses long. I could only see the entire bottom of the craft and just part of the side. I couldn't discern anything about the top of the craft. It appeared to be a gray metallic in color, but of course, the cloudy conditions could have darkened the UFO.

On the bottom of this Triangular craft were two glass-looking globes in the front tip of the triangle. They seemed to be made out of an old glass, similar to that in old factories that covered the light bulbs. These globes were about 6 feet wide and 15 feet long, hanging down from the front of Triangle. Typically, they would have been filled with light because most Triangle crafts have three bright lights on all triangle tips, as people have seen numerous times. I found this craft structure with the glass globes to be different from observations of other Triangle sightings. *This is a rare find*, I thought to myself. Down the center of the Triangle was a grooved-out area about three feet deep, sixty feet long, and 20 feet wide. Towards the back of the UFO, a round vent apparatus with slats, like that of a large grill, was going across the thirty-foot diameter venting system. It made a slight buzzing, hissing sound, not very loud. On the back of the Triangle, both ends of the Triangle tips had these bright lights that I would contend are the propulsion system. The front glass globes were not lit because they did not need the thrust at 30 MPG. On the very back of Triangle, there was a small red-light blinking. This was the largest flying craft I have ever seen. Exhilarating? Yes. I was in awe of this Triangle craft.

The craft flew right over my house, picked up speed, and sped off to the south into the clouds. It made a louder hissing sound upon acceleration as it flew away out of sight. The grill vent area has also been red in most sightings of this Triangle. My reasoning for this is the more power the Triangle uses, the hotter the vent and the redder it turns.

I immediately called my mother, who lived three houses down from me on the street. I was sure she would have seen this large Triangle craft passing over our homes. Though my mother was 84 years old at the time, and she was very mentally alert for her age.

"Did I see it?" She asked, and then exclaimed, "My God, it was big."

My mother told me it passed right over her house. From what I could tell when I was outside, the left tip of the Triangle had passed over her home. As large as it was, it would make all the neighbors think it went over them. She told me she did not go out on the porch because she was afraid of being abducted. So, she viewed it from the large picture windows at the back of the house. My two other brothers were also there with her and had also witnessed the whole Triangle sighting. She insisted that none of them went out to the porch. She was also confident that no other neighbors were looking outside at that time, though the neighbors had expressed interest in seeing this type of UFO and felt terrible about missing it. My mother said the Triangle craft came close to her trees in the front yard. My two brothers were excited and scared while witnessing this UFO. There were four witnesses to this Triangle craft – all family. My mother and two brothers were afraid of the nuclear energy from the ship, but if that were the case, I would be dead by now.

After this Triangle craft's visit, my tree and the neighbor's tree were dead at the top from where the craft passed close by to them. My mother told me that her bushes started dying after the ship passed over them. It brings about the question: Do these types of UFOs have radiation coming off their propulsion anti-gravity systems? It was no coincidence that the Triangle craft passed over my mom, brothers, and myself and it seemed targeted because it was dead center in my driveway. There have been other ships passing over me in the past and delivered an eerie message for me, but I am not sure what it is.

I called the Sheriff's office in Edwardsville, Illinois, and reported the Triangle craft. The dispatcher relayed that nobody had reported a sighting of this Triangle. I asked her not to laugh at me.

"Oh no, we don't laugh at people reporting UFO sightings." She responded. She noted several officers were in the room, and they were interested and not laughing. She shared that her officers had seen several UFO sightings and took it seriously.

The Triangle craft passing right over me and making me feel acknowledged made me think the ETs were communicating with me. My mother said she was afraid of abduction. That said a lot to me about her experiences and her knowledge about abduction at her age.

7

SHORT GREY ET BY BEDSIDE

We never know the time or the place we will encounter an ET or UFO. That is why most people are not prepared with cameras and testing equipment. It is the most minor expected encounter when it happens early in the morning and you are asleep. The following experience was very shocking.

It was back in 1995 when I had my first face-to-face encounter with an ET. It was 2 AM and my wife and I were in bed asleep. I was awakened when I heard a slight noise. As an ex-combat Vet, I can quickly pick up sounds. I sat up and put my chin in my right hand, leaning on my elbow. Sometimes my daughter would come through our bedroom to go to the main bathroom for aspirin for headaches. Thinking this was the case, I called out her name several times and got no answer. It was then I saw a shadow move across our mirror and called out my daughter's name again, still no response. It was very dark in our bedroom, my wife liked to keep it that way so she could sleep better.

The shadow continued around the end of the bed and started towards me. I then put my chin in my left hand and leaned on my elbow, looking towards the shadow. I called out my daughter's name one last time; again, no response. It was then that I felt strange energy next to me in bed, and the shadow revealed itself. I first turned to look at this thing and saw a short grey ET standing next to my bed. We were face-to-face, only a foot or so away from one another. This tiny ET was three and a half feet tall and stood about a foot above our high bed. He caught my gaze and stared at me. He did not have his dark eye coverings, and I could easily see the whites of his eyes. His eyes looked like our eyes except for them being slightly larger. The eye irises were dark in color with a white sclera. The ET was able to paralyze me with his eyes by starring at me. I felt fear for about six seconds during this initial contact, with chills running up and down my body and I was able to get a close look at him before passing out. This ET did not look smooth-skinned like the commercial or movie greys they portrayed. He was very wrinkled, with prominent wrinkles on his forehead. I could not see his ears at all. His nose was just two holes slightly raised, and his mouth was just a tiny slit. The ET's skin, which I thought was simply grey, was dark green and dark gray mixed in the dim light in the room. I started feeling peaceful and calm from his energy. After that, I was put in sleep mode by the ET. I don't remember a thing after that point.

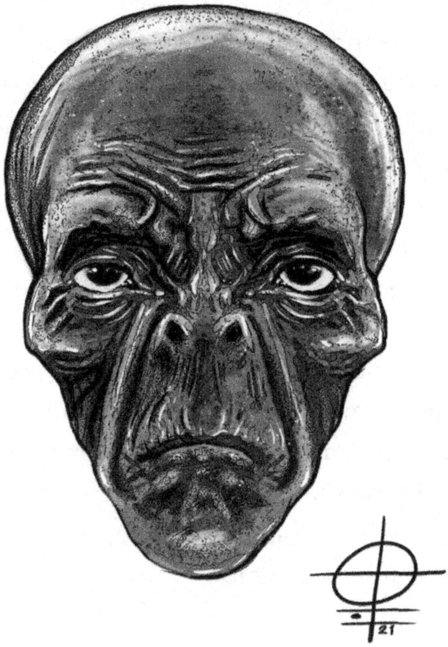

I woke up, it seemed, over an hour later after the ET encounter, close to 3:30 am as far as I can remember. I was dizzy and sleepy, still trying to wake up from the dumbing down.

I shook my wife awake, "Did you see anything?"

"No," she responded groggily.

"You didn't hear any noises?"

"No," She said, turning over, "go back to sleep."

Instead, I went to the bathroom to splash my face with water because my eyes were twitching and blinking like I had a nervous tick. It took a while for my eyes to stop blinking. I had to work early that morning, so I watched TV until work time rather than going back to sleep. I was too excited after that ET encounter to even consider it.

I never did not talk about this ET encounter very much, only to my family and wife. This was shocking because I knew the ETs returned after a few years of no visits or contact. Do I know what this little grey creature did to me? Yes! After looking at the dates of past and future encounters, some of my ET encounters and UFOs seemed to be linked to other ET activities. In this particular instance, the ET took semen and DNA samples and undoubtedly implanted me with implants. They will sometimes do a bodily exam and measure the frequencies of your DNA to make sure they have a healthy semen sample. This grey's sample taking will turn up in the future as offspring hybrids. Notes and timing are essential to keep on these encounters.

8

THE MOTHER SHIP'S VISIT WITH A TALL WHITE HUMANOID WOMAN

In September 2010, I experience a regressed lucid dream, in the early hours of the morning. This lucid dream was an abduction taking my soul, consciousness, and spiritual essence. It was completely unforgettable. This is the lucid dream that the ETs gave me the knowledge of what takes place on large mother ships (which I called *Noah's Arc*). This is not the first lucid dream I've experienced, as I've mentioned before. I have had several lucid dreams that were so real, and in which I understood a seed was planted during several abductions I have been through. Abductions and lucid dreams are not usually timed correctly, or maybe more succinctly, they don't happen in real-time. The lucid dream I'm going to discuss was a time when a regression and abduction co-occurred. That is why talking about it as an ET event in real-time is essential. Most of my lucid dreams don't fit this category.

At the time, I thought to myself, *this has to be dimensional travel.* But, we don't know how the ETs take us to strange places. Some regressions you can't make up, and this is one of them.

In my regression, I found myself standing in the middle of a large hallway about 15 feet wide and ten feet tall—all shiny metallic walls with a grooved stiff fiber light tan color floor. The lighting was a non-intrusive white light that was evenly lit throughout the craft. It did not feel hot or cold inside the craft, on the contrary it was quite comfortable. This was rooted in whether I was in an avatar form or physical. I ventured off, exploring the ship. As I walked down the hall, I saw several small office-type rooms with tables. There were humanoid figures sitting at the desk, but no faces were shown to me. Sometimes this happens in dimensional encounters for some reason, which is why I am not sure if this was dimensional travel assisted by ETs. I walked to the end of the hallway where it opened up to a sizeable convention-type room. Within that room, tall humanoid figures were standing and watching some demonstration. I could not make out the people in the crowd, but there were a lot of humanoid beings. They were looking at three podiums standing above the crowd. A humanoid entity along with an animal on a chain next to them stood on each platform. On the closest platform to me, I could see what I thought to be a humanoid holding a half kangaroo, half monkey-like creature. From this, I got the impression that they were creating life forms for other planets that would match their livable environments. This is when I realized this was a Noah's Arc-type craft. My opinion about the Biblical Noah is that he also had a ship that had all the animals and lifeforms of earth onboard his craft. Maybe this is one of the messages I received was that Noah had the same setup.

As I started back up the hallway from the convention room, I noticed a small black box traveling alongside my right foot. It was 12 inches by 12 inches square and moved with me wherever I walked. Through seemingly telepathic communications I was directed where to go on the ship. Eventually I came upon three women humanoid entities about my height, around 5'10" tall. They were wearing white heavy-looking smocks with their heads covered in a hood. Maybe these were human workers onboard the ship working for the tall whites. The tall whites and Anunnaki created us through DNA manipulation to do their work for them. It could be a correlation to what I saw. I moved in between the three women and looked at what they were doing. What I saw was a human-like baby, about six months old with light skin and three eyes straight across its forehead. I was surprised, to say the least, seeing this three-eyed baby. Did this mean the third eye was an improved human being they were working with that would be more intelligent? Or was this one of the giant's offspring from ancient times? The eyes were straight across the brow, not in the middle of the forehead as we have seen with cyclops. The baby's head was slightly larger than our human heads but not freakish looking. The eyes were blue. I am still trying to figure out the message imparted on me about this baby. Was this my hybrid offspring? Or is this telling me about the third eye being critical to expanded knowledge?

Movement down the hallway caught my attention when I turned away from the caretakers attending to the baby. There was this tall humanoid woman about seven feet tall. She had a bald head – no hair. As she got closer to me, I noticed she was wearing a two-piece outfit. A top covered her chest, and the bottom was like a mini skirt, almost like a two-piece swimming suit. They both were light brown tan in color. She had about a foot of bare stomach area showing. Her shoes were light color brown short high heels that were ankle-high boots. This humanoid woman had large eyes but not much larger than our human eyes. They were greenish, and she had an attractive face. Her skin was ashen with a light complexion but again still not too far removed from a human woman. She did not look threatening, and that calmed my fears. I felt entirely relaxed through this whole adventure on this craft.

Telepathically, she gave me instructions to follow her over to a panel about ten feet away. There was a wall with round shiny metal protrusions sticking out. These protrusions looked like the same metallic shiny metal the walls were made of with no dials, no gauges, no needle pointers, and lights for the controls. There were four protrusions that stuck out about two inches from the wall. As she reached for the control protrusion, I saw her arm, and it had short fine hairs on it. Maybe I was directed to look at her arm to show me they were humanoid like us. When she reached out to touch one of the protrusions, she disappeared momentarily. After a couple of seconds, she came back from being invisible.

"How did you do that?" I asked her.

I was surprised that she acknowledged my question by grimacing her lower lip, which was all she responded with. Back in her physical form, she telepathically told me to follow her. She reached for another control protrusion on-wall and touched it with the whole palm of her right hand.

She turned to an opening just feet away from the control wall. It was a hallway about six feet wide and ten feet in height, which she told me to follow her down. As she walked into the hallway, she slowly disappeared. After that, I followed her, and I was returned to my bed. I woke up, excited by the vivid dream experience. From my experiences, it seems teleportation is their perferred mode of travel.

Maybe this could confuse us with dimensional portals? If I had to mention what race of ETs this woman was, it would be the tall whites. This was a very spiritual pleasant visit to this spaceship. And as for the black square box at my right foot? That was a container for my soul as they put me in a holographic form using only my energy, mind, and consciousness.

9

QUICK VISITS BY REPTILIAN ETS

In November of 2011, I woke up at 4:30 AM to go to the bathroom. I saw a figure in the darkness on the north side of my bed near my closet doors. It seemed to be swaying back and forth, and I think this motion caught my attention. The first thing that came to mind was that a snake sways back and forth, concentrating on prey. I got out of bed to take a closer look at this object, my eyes blurry from sleep. As I got closer, I saw what looked like a five-and-a-half-foot-tall Reptilian ET. It had a large head that looked like a cobra snake. The Head was partially fanned out, it seemed, or it was just the size of its head that confused me in the dark. Unfortunately, it was too dark in the room for me to perceive accurate details. This reptilian seemed to be a dark green using the room's darkness to blend in, making it darker. The ET had large dark eyes that seemed to be more on the sides of the head, not forward appearing. The mouth was like a cobra's mouth which terrified me. It had rough reptile skin and from what I could tell was pitted with dark freckles. This ET could have been a young reptilian from its small size or it could have been a female reptilian, as far as I know. Nobody knows enough about these entities to make any decisive claims.

As I stood by my bed and looked at this creature, it vanished right in front of me. In a panic, I began searching all over the bedroom for a giant snake. After a moment, I stopped, laughing at myself because I figured a reptilian ET was making a brief visit of five seconds. The message I got from this visit was that they were watching me a lot. Some of my UFOlogist friends told me the reptilians make short visits to humans not to scare us but simply to let us know they are watching us. That since they know their appearance is the scariest to us humans, out of most all ETs, they make brief visits or shapeshift into human beings to ease those fears and anxieties about them. From what I know, it is the reptilians are the ETs that shapeshift the most.

If you investigate ancient Egyptian cultures, the King and Queen were most likely reptilian shapeshifters. Drawings depict half human and half animal drawn by Egyptian scribes. I have heard other stories from trusted people that they know of shapeshifting ETs. My best guess is that the reptilians do not have a hybrid program for themselves. They extract semen and eggs from humans to develop humans who then become working slaves to do their bidding. Or, a more horrific idea is to raise humans for food, which is scary. My singular observations of reptilians is they are shapeshifters that can turn into humans anytime they need to. What else would they need us humans for? I heard a story on Howard Stern that caught my curiosity since I am a musician. If anybody likes Metal music, especially the group "Metallica" you are in for a surprise. One of the guitar players told Howard Stern that he knows a reptilian shapeshifter right on the radio. He said it was a woman he knew. Howard said, tell me now. The guitar player said he wouldn't now but would off the air. Howard said alright, I want you to keep your word. Reptilians have been accused of silently leading the deep state Cabal and are evil. I won't guess on that idea at all.

My close call with a Reptilian Shapeshifter

An experience occurred to me in September of 2011 at a club my brothers and I were to perform at with our band. Prior to performing, we went to speak to the club manager about a musical contract. Inside the club were several young ladies in their 20s all dressed up as though they came from a wedding party. One of the young ladies went over to the jukebox to play a Michael Jackson dance song. She wore a long black dress, and she danced like a professional dancer almost floating across the floor. She had long dark hair and green eyes – very attractive. She was about five foot, five inches tall. As she danced, she kept her eyes on me where I was seated with my two younger brothers at a table. As she was dancing around all the barstools, she made her way over to us. She had her hands out as she approached us, giving a "come to me" jester with her fingers, palms up. She came within three feet of me, looking at me in a very sultry way. I turned to my brothers, who were younger and better looking than me.

"What's going on here? You two are younger and better-looking. Why did she motion me on?" I said in disbelief.

She walked back to her friends and was quiet amongst her friends. I felt strange energy but not the aggressive energy a man has when wanting to capture a young lady's attention. It was an energy of curiosity about who she was in real life. She must have read my aura. In the past, I have had guys tell me about strange, beautiful young ladies who seduced them. Auras are a spiritual science to humans, but they are fundamental to hybrids and shapeshifters. They pick their unsuspecting men by the color of their auras. Green is the best aura, while black is the worst aura, with blue and yellow auras somewhere in between. They pick men based on energy, seduce them into bed, and get their semen for hybridizing.

This story of the attractive young lady is particularly interesting to me because of a follow-up encounter I experience about a week later. My brother and I returned to the club to conclude our contract with the club manager. We sat at the bar, and next to me, a stool away was the same dancing young lady from a week earlier in denim pants and a T-shirt.

I turned to my brother, "Is that the same dancing young lady from last week?"

"It seems like it." He glanced over at her. When I turned to look at her without turning her head, she turned her right eye to me. She showed me the reptilian green slit iris, letting me know who she was – a reptilian shapeshifter. I got chills up and down my spine.

"Do you see her eyes? They look like a snakes."

"I can't see them from where I'm sitting." His eyebrows furrowed together, "She is extraordinary though." A shapeshifter will shape themselves into the most attractive person to attract humans to them more easily, and that seemed to be exactly what she had done.

10

A DAY WITH A HUMANOID ET

THE STORY OF HIROKO

I love to travel and take landscape pictures, especially in the southwest of America. Previously while doing so, I was researching the UFO phenomena simultaneously. In October 2010, after the long drive from Illinois to Sedona, Arizona, I got a room at my favorite Lodge. I took a short two-hour nap and went to a restaurant upon waking up. From there, I went to a large gift shop in Sedona near Cathedral Rock. The employees there told me a UFO sighting the night prior at Cathedral Rock.

"Great, I know where Cathedral Rock is. I will go there now." I was excited and left quickly, heading in that direction. When I got to the parking lot of Cathedral Rock, I immediately started filming with my video camera.

It was a cloudy overcast day about to rain, and as I was taking videos of the area of Cathedral Rock, a small white car pulled into the parking space directly behind my vehicle. Out steps a smiling young Asian woman slowly coming up to me. She approached me like a little girl.

"Are you here for a hike or waiting for someone?" I asked her.

"No, I am here to meet you because we were supposed to meet."

She answered. I agreed with her on this point. I kept filming the Cathedral Rock as we spoke and got some film of her.

"Do you believe in UFOs?" I asked. She just looked at me without an answer. I stopped filming and turned my attention to her, "Were we supposed to meet?"

"Yes." She held my gaze.

"Do I know you?"

"Maybe. I don't know you."

"What is your name?"

"Hiroko or you can call me Hero." She gave me a small smile.

I asked again if she planned on going hiking again. She shook her head no.

"Well, it is going to rain. Would you like to get into my car and talk?" I suggested to her. She nodded in response. When she got into my car, I asked her if she was afraid of being with a strange guy.

"No, I'm not," She said.

"You can kick my butt, I guess." I laughed.

"Yes, I can."

That is when I took notice of her energy coming from her dark eyes.

One spot over from my car, another white car was pulling into the parking space. There was a young man, with a close cropped burr haircut, and was around 26 years old, maybe more. He wore a headset on his head with a microphone. If I had to guess he appeared to be a law enforcement official or NSA agent. Not even once did he turn his face to me. That was a red flag to me that he could be involved with Hiroko somehow.

"Hiroko, do you know this man?"

She nervously shook her head, "No."

Any other time, I would be worried about a setup robbery, but with Hiroko's energy being peaceful, I felt relaxed. It was as if she was imploring me to be calm and not become defensive through her eyes. I had a weapon in my car console, and I could tell she knew it by the way she stared at me when I looked at the console.

Hiroko had no watch, no jewelry, and just wore a thin white sweater with mud-splattered denim pants. She had a tank top under the sweater, but as cool and rainy it was at that time, she should have been cold. She claimed she was up on Cathedral Rock, and there was only one person up there with her. The mud splatter on her pants from the night before is not how a young lady wears her clothes. Hiroko had shoulder-length dark hair and a facial bone structure that was not Asian. I could not believe a young lady would not have makeup on or not even have a cell phone with her. This is what alerted me that she was not like us humans, and her behavior was the fundamental characteristic.

Hiroko and I talked about her family and living in Tokyo. Usually, the hybrids and humanoid intra-terrestrials elicit emotional behavior from us humans. They learn our human culture in order to walk among us. I firmly believe that extracting our emotions is what Hiroko was doing to me. She began asking me questions.

"What you would do if a workmate gave you a tough time and did not like you?" She asked.

"I would try to talk it out because fighting at work could get you fired." I told her.

Then she said her mom and dad mistreated her as she grew up. She started crying at that point. I could tell it was a fake cry.

"That is fine, do not feel bad showing emotions." I put my hand on her hand, and was shocked. Her body was extremely hot. It seemed to me to be above any human fever pitch. "You are extremely hot. Are you feeling all right?" I worried.

"Yes, I am fine." Hiroko shrugged.

"Its very cool outside and with truly little clothing, you should be cold."

It was at this time, that the agent-looking guy came back after being gone for 20 minutes. He pulled into the same spot that he left. Again, he did not look at me, and Hiroko just stared at me telepathically; she was telling me not to be alarmed. Normally my military training would have been utilized in a robbery scenario. But Hiroko's eyes kept me dumbed down and peaceful.

Hiroko told me that she knew twenty languages but could not read English. She had me read a page out of a travel booklet for her. I found that to be very odd not being able to read English but being able to speak it. She could read symbols and not the text, as I would guess. Being from a Japanese upbringing or an ET background would allow symbol reading knowledge. The agent-looking guy drove off again without looking at us. I kept thinking he had a listening device on his head. I knew, somehow, this young agent guy and Hiroko had some connection.

We kept talking about her home in Tokyo, but honestly, I did not believe she lived there.

"Do you have siblings in Japan?" I questioned.

"No." She shook her head a little.

Then I asked her a question that told me a lot about who she was.

"How old are you?"

Hiroko stared at me angrily and then snapped, "Why do you people think in age and time? There is no time or age."

To me, that said volumes about who she is. That she is not from here on earth. Her eyes were very dark and piercing at that moment. I told her to stop staring at me because she burned a hole through my head. Her energy dumbed me down because she slumped in her seat, looking much smaller with more enormous eyes, and I was not alarmed by this. It took a few minutes for her to remember to make herself smaller, looking more like a petite grey ET. It did not dawn on me until later when I got back to my room.

The agent-looking guy came back one last time. In total, he came and left three times, always parking in the same spot and never looking around at his surroundings. Each time, Hiroko would stare at me as if saying, *stay calm. No trouble will come to you.* I likely could have been abducted that evening and not known it. As I've mentioned, people don't know if they were abducted, dumbed-down, or under mind control.

As we talked about her and her brief earthly background most of the time, she mentioned she had a boyfriend in Tokyo.

"Will you get married to him?"

"He was mean to me and wanted to break up with me." was her answer. This was said after she said she needed a baby.

"How are you going to have a baby when you are not married?" I wondered.

"I need a baby even if my boyfriend breaks up with me."

This young agent-looking guy took off again for the last time, he had to be monitoring us. I told Hiroko we should go back to our rooms now that it was getting late. I asked her if she wanted to meet for breakfast at 101 omelets café at 9:30 am the next day. Amazingly, she said yes, that would be fine. We got in our cars and took off. Hiroko drove extremely fast; I could not keep up with her.

My thought after our two hours together near Cathedral Rock was that Hiroko was guarded with what she told me and had repeatedly stated, "we were supposed to meet." As I was writing my notes about Hiroko in my room at the lodge, I kept thinking about why she needed a baby. Who was this stranger, and was she an ET? It did not feel as though this was a romantic meeting up. It was possibly a daughter and dad's reunification. I wrote three legal-size pages of notes that night in my room. I felt like a spiritual event had just happened to me with Hiroko. Being with an off-world humanoid ET was a gift.

After both of us agreed, we went our own ways to our rooms that night. I did not recall anything strange until I had a regressed dream a few months after I met Hiroko. This peculiar event that the dream was about occurred several hours later, that night after we parted to our rooms.

This lucid, regressed dream that I recalled about the early morning of the October 5, 2010, event. I was in bed asleep sometime between 2 AM and 4 AM. I noticed somebody or something moving my right leg around. My knee was up, and someone was putting a light brown hose to my crotch area. I remembered trying to kick the hose away with my right knee. After that attempt, they put me back to sleep. The next thing I recognized in this lucid dream was that someone, or something, was holding my left arm at my elbow. Another person or entity I could not see had a bright white light in his hand. This light was about seven inches long and reminded me of a small fluorescent tube. It had a black casing with the light on the front part of the tube turned towards my eyes. They walked me back and forth in my room and kept passing the light over my eyes. The bright light hurt my eyes as it passed over them. I could see two humanoid figures sitting at my room's small table, but they were just dark shadows. I noticed that I was being led up to the sliding doors of the room's exit. They were at least gentle about walking me back and forth. The light was the only pain I felt. I ultimately have no idea how long this memory-erasing went on, but it seems that they did not get all the memory. The reason for this whole event? Semen collection. They had four entities attempting to extract it from me and then they were erasing my memory of what they did to me. But do ETs want you to forget everything or leave enough information to let you know they are in control?

When I woke up around 8 AM in the lodge room, I noticed my blankets were more messed up than usual. I saw a big hint of what occurred earlier that night. There were eight drops of blood on the fitted sheet. I checked myself and did not see any cuts or scratches on my body. I thought, *alright, something to think about as I start my day.* I then took pictures of almost all these strange occurrences. My mind was still in a dumb-down mode, so I was difficult for me to think straight. I got cleaned up and got dressed to meet Hiroko at 9:30 AM at the café. It crossed my mind, the lack of getting adequate sleep the night before, but I brushed it off. The my memory recollection did not happen until later. I recalled again how Hiroko had said several times, "I need a baby."

Hiroko showed up at the Café around 9:45 AM - 15 minutes late. I got messages from her for a strange reason that she would show up telepathically. She pulled in the lot, and I asked her if she was checked out of her room. Hiroko looked at me curiously, and I informed her that she needed to say to the room clerk that she was leaving and that if she didn't they might also charge her the next day if she used a credit card. I gave her my cell phone and helped her with the phone number. Hiroko called her room clerk and cleared her charges up but it seemed to me that somebody else was taking care of her business and had a handler.

While we were in the restaurant in a waiting line, Hiroko observed, "all these people."

This struck me as off because if she was from Tokyo, that city has millions of people on the streets. Often, things she said did not make sense; I guess she thought I did not take note of them. I ordered our breakfast because Hiroko could not read English. Hiroko told me she had only eaten baked pastries in the room she stayed in. There has been research that found ETs eat bread and pastries only. Of course, she was preoccupied with all the people in the Café and did not say much during our breakfast and while she ate very little, I finished my meal. Before we left the restaurant, Hiroko had to go to the lady's room.

After leaving the restaurant, we drove around Sedona to visit all the Buttes. I gave her a bottle water, but she did not drink much. I tried to remember all these little red flags Hiroko was putting out during our conversations. That day she carried a small black canvas-looking bag about 10 inches long. Man, I would have loved to see what she had in the black bag.

We stopped at a Butte and went for a walk on one of the many trails in Sedona. It was muddy after the rain the night before, and I did not want to walk the trail. I saw a creek bed that had mud sediments that looked like milk chocolate and I mentioned it to Hiroko that it looked like chocolate. She bent down and put some mud on her fingers, then licked it and swallowed it.

"You want some to eat?" she asked.

"I think I will pass on eating mud. Thank you."

I then told her wanted to pray for her and her family and to have a baby. I held her hand in prayer, and I spoke the words asking God to bless her. Hiroko did not seem very enthused about the prayer. After she walked out further in the parking lot. She seemed to enjoy the fresh air and scenery.

She spread her arms, "Can you hear the breeze?"

Hiroko seemed like a person that had not been exposed to nature very much. We went to the airport lookout overlooking Sedona. Both of us sat on a large stone together and viewed the scenery. After a few moments, Hiroko spoke.

"I like bluebirds. They are pretty."

As soon as she said that, a bluebird landed in a tree about 30 feet away.

"You're magical, Hiroko," I said, eyeing the bluebird.

We spent about a half-hour at the airport lookout enjoying the view of the city of Sedona. While we were seated on the large rock, a Japanese older gentleman walked past us. He had several cameras and a camera vest on. I remembered the look he gave me as he walked past me, it was just as if he knew me. He gave a quick glance at Hiroko and walked on by us. It felt like Hiroko and the older Japanese Guy knew each other personally.

"Why didn't you say hi to your fellow Japanese countryman?" I questioned Hiroko.

"In the Japanese culture, we don't say hi to one another in other countries because it is rude." she explained. I told her we Americans speak to each other in foreign countries and she did not react. After the older Japanese Guy passed us, I felt again that they knew each other, and felt intuitively that he was her human handler. Humanoid ETs need a human handler to train them in human culture and communications. I believe the young man parked near us the night before with a headset on was her security detail. To me, that was the support group that (Dr. Mack, Dr. Jacobs) and most UFOlogists believe to happen to train ETs for human assimilation.

Eventually, we got back in the car and went to the gift shop I visited just before meeting Hiroko. I told her she needed a souvenir to take with her to remember Sedona. We got to the shop, and I found a necklace with a crystal as an amulet. It had amber beads on it, also with wire designs. I told her that would give her power. Hiroko held it in her hand and started sobbing with tears in her eyes. I felt she was faking a cry to practice human skills.

"I have 'power' now," She cried. "The power comes from Cathedral Rock."

This is where people saw the UFO the night before. It was strange she said that about Cathedral Rock because she visited that Butte several times. I wondered what the connection was to her about Cathedral Rock.

Hiroko told me she had to leave at 3 PM to go to Phoenix to catch a flight to Los Angeles. I suggested we go to a restaurant for lunch before she left. We left the gift shop for a pizza restaurant in town. I ordered two pieces of pizza for both of us, a soda for me, and water for Hiroko.

It was then she repeated the same line she had many times before.

"We were supposed to meet."

"Can you tell me why?" I probed.

She said nothing, just stared at me as usual. We talked a little before our food was brought to our table.

"I like you." She said finally. I met her gaze.

"Your eyes are very piercing, please don't stare at me like that," I implored. "Hiroko, you are strange. Surely you are not an Angel?"

"No, I am not an Angel." She shook her head.

Hiroko did not eat much again but never said anything wrong about food. She went to the lady's room after eating a little pizza. It seemed she went to the lady's room after eating a little food. Hiroko returned to the table and told me again that she liked me a lot.

"I wished I knew who you are," I said softly, "Why do you travel by yourself as a single lady?"

She explained she travels all the time by herself, mentioning that she had been to White Sands, New Mexico, by herself.

"Why you would go to White Sands by yourself?" I questioned.

"To see the white sand."

I found that an unusual answer because if she was an ET, maybe she worked underground with our Military. Was she exchanging technologies? Her saying she just liked the white sand was very strange to me.

We left the restaurant, and as we were talking, she said she was going to Los Angeles because there were many friendly people there. We got back to my room at the lodge where her rental car was parked. That same day, I took a total of nine pictures of us together. I told her I had taken the pictures and asked if she wanted a copy. She requested that I email them to her, to make sure I sent the images as she wished somebody else could see them. She wrote down an email address, "Make sure you send them."

I then gave her my simple name card with phone and email information – no address.

"Goodbye, Hiroko. This has been interesting."

"Goodbye." She responded.

"Can I kiss you goodbye?"

She pointed to her cheek with her finger, so I kissed her on the cheek like a father-daughter kiss. I remember her skin felt thick and not soft like ordinary women. She got in her car and took off fast down the road waving her arm back at me. The car she had looked very stripped down with no bells and whistles. I went to my room and wrote down some notes about our day together. I wrote three pages of notes on Hiroko and my day together. I was dissatisfied because I did not hear the truth about who she was and where she came from. There was a feeling I had that it would not be the last I would hear from her.

I sent the emails I promised Hiroko with our pictures attached in November 2010. I sent two photos at a time on each email. To my surprise, she got the emails, and she replied with her thanks. I asked her how she was doing in the emails. Her initial replies were gloom and doom and she said she was depressed. In my response, I inquired why. Hiroko said, "Your God was not good to me." And continued to say, "Why does your God treat me like this?" My thoughts were she was still emotionally extracting feelings from me. She told me her boyfriend was mean to her, and they broke up. I wrote back to her suggested she talk to someone about her depression. I sent twelve photos to her between November and December 2010. A total of seven emails were exchanged during those two months between us. Since Hiroko could not read English, she had her handlers read them for her. I noticed that there might have been three different people answering the emails because the emails had differences in writing style.

During this time, I had hoped she would tell me who she was – ET. Hiroko's replies seemed like she was distressed. One response from her expressed doubts of her wanting to live any longer. I told her I loved her like a daughter because I felt in some way, she was part of me. I told her not ever to kill herself. Hiroko wrote back and said, "I am OK." This all seemed like a game of emotions she was playing with me. Hiroko learned human emotions by communicating her false feelings in our email exchanges. After receiving all the photos, she said, "just leave me alone." I responded with a last-ditch effort to get her to say she was an ET. I told her in another reply that I thought she was an alien hybrid, and the strange young guy with the headset was her security, maybe NSA. Finally, I told her the older Japanese gentleman we met on Airport Lookout was her human sponsor. Hiroko did reply to this accusation but differently than I expected.

"God gave me a gift, and I will not be lonely any longer."

My thoughts were she got the baby she wanted. I had difficulty figuring out how she got her baby because it was only two months since we last met. Our last email contact was December 27, 2010. I have all the email exchanges on my files for the note ledger. After the night of the intruders in my lodge room, which took semen samples from my groin area, I wondered if that was my baby as that was the day I met Hiroko for the first time.

I had the feeling this Hiroko story was not over for some reason. Usually, I wait until all the facts are in before I conclude any experience. The following will prove that Hiroko was a real humanoid ET.

The second part of the story of Hiroko starts up again on March 17, 2011, at 1:30 PM. It was a warm St. Patrick's Day in Godfrey, Illinois. My cousin R was sitting on my front porch smoking cigars and enjoying the nice day. It has been almost six months since Hiroko and I met in Sedona, Arizona. My cousin and I saw three Asian people standing up the road from us, about two hundred fifty feet away. They seemed to appear out of nowhere, catching both of us off guard—all three of the Asian people starting walking towards us.

"Do you know those Chinese people?" My cousin asked, peering down at them.

"I think so." I said, "And they are Japanese, not Chinese."

As they approached us, the female stopped and turned her back.

"I think I know the woman standing with her back against us." I told my cousin.

The two young men walked up to my driveway and stopped about ten feet away from my cousin and me. They were teenagers, wearing very colorful clothing and tennis shoes. One was about fifteen and the other around seventeen years old. The older young man was six feet tall, and the other young boy was about five feet ten inches tall. They stopped, staring at us with dark eyes and a look of curiosity.

Deep inside, I knew the young woman standing about one hundred twenty-five feet away from us was Hiroko. She had on the same denim jeans and a thin white sweater, standing with her arms folded. This was the same stance she had in Sedona. The two young men were taller than average young Japanese young men. Their cheekbones were more prominent than other Japanese young men.

Reminded me of Hiroko's facial structure. As my cousin and I sat quietly, the older young man, called out to us.

"Do you know where the new Walmart is?"

"It's just over the highway overpass about a quarter of a mile." I answered.

The taller, older young man did not say anything in reply. After that, neither my cousin nor me could talk. We were dumbed down where we could not speak. I wanted to ask them if that was Hiroko down the road from us. I could not get the words out of my mouth. My cousin was glassy-eyed, looking to the floor, and unable to speak. My cousin is usually a big communicator and talks to everybody. But he was not saying anything, just like me.

I remember I was able to look around but could not speak. I saw the taller young man look at me intently with his dark eyes. The younger of the two had a nervous tick in his right leg that he kept shaking like this was his first experience talking to other people. They both were looking at me primarily. My cousin was really in a deep sleep and not noticing anything. The taller boy must have gone past me and into my house to get my notes case I carried on my travels. He looked at me while he was inspecting my case of notes, and I thought, *what is this all about?* I did not see him walk past me twice into my house, and I thought this was crazy. The notecase had a lot of notes on (his mother) Hiroko while in Sedona. I did not notice at the time, but this young man took some of my notes on Hiroko when I remembered to inspect my notecase. Luckily, I had a typed ledger of the same notes, and I won't forget this experience with Hiroko. It is a very spooky feeling when you are under mental control by someone else. This was in broad daylight, and we could not get control of our minds and bodies.

When I looked up the road at who I knew was Hiroko, the taller young man gave me a mean look. He was reading my mind, and he sensed I knew it was Hiroko I was staring at. They both were reading our minds. During that time, Hiroko could have come up to the porch. We would not have known. My cousin and I did not know how long they controlled us. The taller young man must have returned my notecase because he did not have it in his hands when they turned to join Hiroko up the road. When the two young men crossed my street, heading towards Hiroko, I started coming to my senses. My cousin woke up when they were close to Hiroko, as they were joining up with her.

"When did you see them start walking away?" My cousin asked.

"After they crossed my street, maybe fifty feet away." I responded

"What the hell happened, Dave?"

"Let us watch where they go."

My cousin started cursing about what had happened. I tried to ease his anxieties by telling him I would explain later. We watched them go up to the highway stop sign where they started altogether. As we watched them, they stood still by the stop sign and just took one second to look back, and they were gone. We both had a full view of the highway up and down the road. The three visitors did not walk up the highway or down the highway. Just like they came, we did not see them appear at the stop sign or leave from the stop sign. They had to have been beamed up or teleported back to their invisible UFO craft.

My cousin got up, "Those ETs will kill you one of these days if you keep messing with them. I am getting the hell out of here. This is scary stuff. See you later."

My cousin got in his truck and sped off. I spoke to his wife the next day, and she told me he was shaken up over that incident. When I started to explain the encounter to her, she said, "I don't want to hear about the incident. Your cousin told me all I need to know."

The next day my cousin called me and said he heard a humming sound like a diesel motor idling in his neighborhood. He looked all over his street at 3 AM.

"It's the Taos HUM." I told him.

"What is that sound?" He asked, perplexed.

"It's a low-frequency sound around 20hrtz or lower. It's beyond human hearing, but there are a lot of people who can hear this HUM."

It was strange my cousin got the HUM the next day after the ET encounter at my house. The other unusual thing was, I think that is when I got my implant in my left leg shin. I dug out the implant a few months later. Three weeks after Hiroko's visit, a large triangle craft flew over my house. Do these things add up? Not sure, but it is a synchronicity effect.

My other conclusion was that these two young Japanese men were Hiroko's offspring. I would also have to say they were part of my DNA. Hiroko brought them to see me only once. Most experiencers say they see their offspring hybrid kids one time, and that is all. But how did she find my house? The card I gave her had only my phone and name on it, and I had to physically write the email address on that card. No address was ever given to her.

11

BLUE ALIEN HYBRID

On July 17, 2010, I had a lucid dream, a regressed dream from previous abductions early in the morning. That is why I feel this is important enough to classify this dream as an alien event.

I dreamed I again was on another planet in a craft that I felt I had been on board before. I was standing in a laboratory area when I arrived at the craft. There was a hallway about six feet wide and nine feet high that I was standing next to. This is where I was transported into the craft. There were the same stainless steel-looking walls and rough fiber floors that I have seen on UFO crafts before. Additionally, there was a glassed-in portion of the lab that looked like an office where an older, blue-spotted male ET stood. He was a blue ET hybrid. He touched the wall protrusions to open a door. The protrusions did not have dials, lights, or buttons, just small round six-inch in diameter touch control with same metallic makeup as the walls as I had seen before.

I did not see this blue-spotted ET's face. I saw only his arm, which had little hairs and blue spots. This ET was wearing a long white medical type of outer garment. He motioned and telepathically told me to lay down on the floor. A long dark-haired woman covered in a light white blanket was on the floor. She was in a fetal position, and I never saw her face either. She looked to me to be human-looking with tanned skin. This elder ET lifted the blanket and told me telepathically to get behind the woman. I can tell he was an elder because of the telepathic thoughts.

The blue hybrid instructed me telepathically to make love to her and copulate for reproduction purposes. It felt like it was real in the mating process. He telepathically told me to get up and follow him to the hallway. The ET touched a couple of circular wall protrusions. Then he led me into the hallway. It seemed my abduction was for this one purpose with the dark-haired woman. I do not remember taking off the sleepwear from my body or putting it back on. I was abducted from bed so that I would have had on shorts and a T-shirt. Blue hybrid told me to walk down the hallway slowly telepathically. As I walked down the transporter hallway, I felt myself disappearing slowly. I ended up back in bed, wide awake from what just happened to me. I found my magnetic bracelet lying on the floor close to my bed. This bracelet is tough to remove, even in the ordinary wearing of the bracelet. The transporter would not have liked the magnetic metal bracelet.

Truthfully, it is difficult to match the abduction with the regressed event in a lucid dream. The time and place of the abduction is also tough to figure out. That is why there is no solid natural science with experiencer's events. ETs want to keep us off the truth of what they are doing. You can remember only as much as they want you to know. They know that without conclusive facts, the disinformation amongst us humans on a person's validity of their experiences is somewhat humiliating.

12

DIMENSIONAL ENTITIES

THE OLD COWBOY

It was October 5, 2010, and it was the rainy season in Sedona. That same evening in Sedona, Arizona, I left after Hiroko left for the airport earlier. The rain being with us for a while gave me a reason for going. Sedona, unfortunately, is not pretty in the rain. I packed my bags and loaded the car. Just before I stepped into my car, I heard a voice say, "I wouldn't leave right now if I were you." I looked around and saw an older man dressed in old cowboy clothes with cowboy boots and suspenders looked like he was from the 1880s. He wore an old beat-up dirty small cowboy hat. He was a small man with a stubbly beard and a dirty-looking long sleeve shirt. His face was well weathered with wrinkles, but he had a friendly smile on his face.

The old man was puffing on a tobacco pipe as he repeated the words, "I would not leave now if I were you."

The weatherman on TV had said the bad weather was going west of Flagstaff. So, I should have been safe traveling on I-40 east toward New Mexico. But the old man stuck to his words, "Do not leave now, stay another night."

I started leaving anyway, not heeding the older man's words of warning. As the older man rocked in a rocking chair and smoked his pipe, he just stared at me as I started to drive off. I got to Flagstaff and turned east to New Mexico which is precisely when I found out the old-timer was right. I ran into a hailstorm with large tennis ball size hail and terrible winds. I looked up and saw an ugly rotating cloud above the highway on the interstate. It was a scary drive for about an hour. I chastised myself, thinking I should have listened to the older man's warning. That day there were five tornadoes in Arizona, and around the Flagstaff area was the first tornado in fifty years.

I remembered when I left the lodge, I looked back, and the older man was not there. He and the rocking chair was gone. I thought the old guy was a dimensional entity because he was out of place with his clothing. There was no rocking chair on the porch of the Lodge. Plus, the older man knew something futuristic and gave me a warning. Somewhat Like an Angel would. I felt the energy off the older man was from the 1880s when he spoke to me, but I did not react appropriately because I was packed and ready to leave.

Just like the spiritual guide told me, I ended up with car damage but finish my trip. The car had $2,600.00 worth of hail damage. This same spiritual guide lady told me I would see my first ET on the 4th of October 2010, during my travels. This spiritual lady was four for five predictions correct overall. It seems the ETs probing my subconscious opened a pathway for my third eye to see dimensional entities.

Little Blonde Girl on a Leash

I loved traveling to Sedona, Arizona, because of the subtle energies it possesses. I did not know what I would find next in this beautiful City. My second trip to Sedona was in May 2010, and each time, I knew something of mystery would show up.

I was sitting on a log bench outside my room, relaxing and smoking a cigar when I saw this 1957 Chevy station wagon light green and white two-tone colors pull in the lot near the Lodge office. A woman was driving, and she got out of the car to go to the office. She was dressed as though she had just jumped out of the 1950s. She was about early thirties with long blonde hair. She was wearing a long colorful skirt and a white blouse. Then a man about six feet 2 inches tall of medium build with a burr haircut in his early thirties of age got out of the car. He, too, was dressed in a short-sleeve white shirt with khaki pants. He got out of the passenger side of the vehicle. He opened the back door and reached for a little girl wearing a 1950s puffed-up dress and the top attached to the dress. She wore a light blue outfit with white shoes. The shocking part of this threesome was that the little girl was on a jewel-studded dog leash. The father held the leash and guided her about twelve feet from my bench to the other bench. The guy sat down and acted like he was reading a pamphlet. His wife was still in the office.

The little girl was about five years old or younger. She was very pale, with short-cropped blonde hair and sparkling little blue eyes. I heard a dog barking out of nowhere, but no dog was around. Then I saw the little girl dragging her feet in the rocks and barking simultaneously. This little girl barked better than most dogs. She looked at me and barked at me. Her face was the only face I saw from the three of them. My conclusion is that they don't show their face in most dimensional events. I was surprised by these events but did not move to speak or go over to them at the bench. The girl barked several more times at me and then stopped.

There is always an energy around dimensional events, like being dumbed down and not reacting to the situation. This guy didn't look at me, not even one time, in the face and I never saw his wife come back out of the lodge office. I got up and went to my room to freshen up for dinner. I sat down on the bed and quickly came to my senses. I guess the dimensional magnetism wore off. I got up and walked out to where those two were on the porch. The little girl was never allowed to sit on the bench from all appearances. They were all gone by the time I got outside. It only took 3 minutes for me to decide. I would tell the guy holding the colorful leash to take the little girl off the leash, or I would call the cops. It is against the law to have a leash around a kid's neck. But it was a time jump or dimensional slip took me in. I was temporarily caught up in their time, in the 1950s, in the fog of dimensional energy.

I went to the office and asked John, the manager, if he saw a little girl on a leash and a couple checking in for a room.

"No, did you see them?" He tilted his head to the side.

"I saw them." I was adamant.

"Don't get spooked by this; people see these types of dimensional things here in Sedona a lot." He gave me a reassuring smile, and went back to what he was working on. I expressed my thanks to him. I had thought I was seeing things that were not there.

Dimensional Travel to another Planet

Back in 2008, I had a dimensional experience different from the usual abductions. Within the UFO community, in all our joint research, we can't tell if the body goes to another location or if it is our spirit, souls, and consciousness that leaves the body for travel. ETs can use portals for traveling to other dimensions like our dimension. On this occasion, it could have been a regressed dream, possibly from my early UFO abductions.

This particular instance, I felt a surge of energy in my body while I was in bed trying to sleep. At that point, I felt like I was asleep but traveling upwards through the roof. I ended up in a small apartment with other young humanoid kids my age in the early teens. We were trying to play music, and my drum parts on earth looked different than what these drums looked. The hardware for these had only two metal support arms for holding a drum, whereas our earthly drums had three components. We just played around for a couple of minutes; then we went outside. The small apartments looked like a worker's camp facility. Again, I did not see their faces, just their bodies. We all went to a supply yard, and I ended up sitting on a pile of lumber. Beside me was a young girl that I spoke a few words, but it seemed she did not understand. Her face I could see, and she looked like a typical young girl with short light brown hair. She had dark brown eyes and was very thin. I looked around at the scenery, and it almost appeared earthlike. The work camp was close to a large river flowing right by the mining camp. I looked at the sky, and I could see two suns not too far apart from one another. It seemed the camp was in a valley. There were hills to one side with evergreen trees just like here on earth. It seemed like I was in our northwest area of the U.S. It was fantastic weather and easy for me to breathe, so it had to be similar to our earth. I kept looking at the two suns because that was different than our planet. People always say when you see two suns, you are on another planet.

I saw men coming up the steps out of the mine shaft. They were dirty, like they had been digging for a dark black tar substance. Dressed in thick clothing blackened by the tar substance, they wore helmets with shields on them. I sat there with the little girl while other young humanoids ran around the supply yard. I asked her, and this was a strange question, proving I was on another planet, "Do you believe in God?"

I still don't think she understood my English because she just looked at me. Her gaze drifted over my head, and I turned to see what she was looking at. A tall male humanoid dressed in all black with a long black coat was standing watching us. When I looked over at him, he was motioning for me to come to the walkway where he was standing. First, I looked at the men coming up from the mine, and I could swear one man looked like my dad with a blackened face, who had passed in 1995. He did not look happy. *What was this place?* I asked myself.

I started walking towards the man in black, and I looked down and saw two colorful three-inch-long toy figures of two animals on the ground. I picked them up and put them in my pocket. Finally, I thought I got some facts that I was here on this planet. When I was next to the man in black, he stretched his arm out and telepathically told me to walk down the wooden walkway. As I walked, I felt myself moving fast to some other place. I ended up in my bed wide awake and excited. I reached for my pockets in my sleeping shorts to retrieve the toy figurines, but they were not there. I felt terrible because I thought I would have another world's toys for proof of travel to another planet.

This is not my first out-of-body-travel through dimensions but one of the most intriguing. ETs will leave you with an expanded consciousness when they go deep into your subconscious. ETs work on our subconscious and have control of our thoughts. That is why they can put us to sleep, erase memories, and give us visions of the past and future.

13

BODY DOUBLES AND CLONES

We speak of body doubles as made or crafted by human hands in modern times. If you get someone who looks nearly like a person physically with modern makeup techniques, you can almost make a copy of that person. Then there is the scientific laboratory process that can produce a clone by splicing DNA and manipulating female eggs and male sperm. There has been a lot of success making cloned animals. But could scientists, unbeknownst to the general public, successfully cloned a human? The possibilities are very likely it has been done already. Does the military have the science to reproduce a human and make a super soldier? There is a lot of disinformation in the conspiracy news that says Hollywood stars have body doubles. Worse of all, there are politicians who have replicas that periodically sit in for the real politician. In my experiences, I feel ETs perform body doubling to "walk amongst us." This author's opinion is that all the above-stated cloning procedures do exist. The following events are actual and witnessed by others.

I traveled through New Mexico and passed the Trinity Nuclear test site area. Those who know Smokey the Bear, know he is the symbol for being careful with campfires and protecting our forest from wildfires. This was his hometown and burial site that I passed by. The two-lane highway was immaculate and looked new—no rocks or debris in the road and there were no other cars around. About two miles east of Smokey's burial site, I heard a loud thump on the passenger side of the car window. I slowed down and looked for damage but found nothing. I remember chills going up to my back and neck. I felt something was with me in my car, and I could feel the energy. I drove very slowly and watched for anything that would produce the thump sound. About five minutes later, I heard the thump on the passenger's glass window again. This time it seemed to go out of the window, rather than in. This made me believe this could be energy coming and going after its mission was accomplished. I checked all my car operation lights and the time, and I found everything okay. But I was still tingling from the mystery energy that came into my car.

After the excitement of the energy in the car, I headed for Roswell, New Mexico. I got there a couple of hours later and checked into my room. Then, I toured around Roswell, and the famous Hanger Eighteen is an avionics parts storeroom. I did not see or hear anything special in Roswell, so I left for San Antonio, Texas. The only strange happening was that I felt I had lost another hour. My brother Jack called me continuely to keep track of my travels due to his fear of me being taken by ET due to my ET experiences and because I was traveling alone.

On June 5,2010, I arrived in San Antonio, Texas at around 7:30 pm and checked into the Quality Inn to stay one night. I talked to the receptionist for about thirty minutes. She told me about her parents seeing UFOs after I explained I was trying to get pictures of UFOs out west. The receptionist seemed nice and was good at her job. I asked her for recommendations on where I could go for dinner. She told me to go across the interstate where there were several restaurants. I went to dinner and returned to my room around 10 PM that evening. I was tired and had to put antibiotic cream on my leg from a fall I had out of my car in New Mexico. I cleaned up, took ibuprofen, and fell asleep at 10:30 PM, exhausted from all the driving and my leg hurting.

The next day around 9 AM, I went to the motel office to check out of my room. It was the same receptionist that checked me in the night before.

"Are you working back-to-back shifts?" I asked her.

"Yes." She responded very angrily.

"What's wrong?" I was bewildered by her anger.

"You know."

"No, I don't know."

"I saw you last night at the Walmart in town at 11:30 PM. You were following me around the store." She snapped.

I laughed, "I was sleeping in bed at that time."

"No, it was you for sure. You had the same clothes that you had on last night and it looked exactly like you."

"There's no way that was me."

She became more more agitated as we talked. So, I gave up and asked for my receipt because I was getting upset by her insistence that it was me. I wanted to tell the manager about her attitude towards me. But then I thought I was simply a guy from out of town, so I walked backward out the door, calling the receptionist a liar as I exited. I got in my car and left and thought to myself, *this was crazy*. I recalled the energy from the day before, and my curiosity told me there was a connection with this double of me.

After San Antonio, I went to Houston for a few days to see my friends. After three days of having a good time with them, I left for St. Louis, Missouri region. When I got home in Illinois, I figured I better get my car serviced after a long trip. On June 10, 2010, I took my car to my dealer for a routine checkup. I had been sitting in my chair for only a few minutes when a guy who looked like he had just finished playing golf walked over to me.

"You have been here for two hours, Buddy." He said to me.

I shook my head, "No, I just got here.:

"I don't want to get into particulars about you, but I have seen you sitting in this same place for over two hours."

"It was not me sitting here, Mister."

He looked at me angrily and said, "I have had enough of this crap." He walked away abruptly.

He seemed like a very intelligent man, but I was glad he was away from me. At this point, this incident and the double incident in Texas scared me. In journalism, you wait for the facts to fall to support the initial story. Well, this incident clarified my thoughts of having a double. *This*, I thought right away, *was done by my ET*.

Back in the 1500s, in Scandinavia, they talked of body doubles that they called *Vardage* or *Doppelgänger*. These people looked like another person. They spoke like the person and wore the same clothes as the person. Since I believe that ETs have been around for thousands of years here on earth, I figured that must have been their doing. ETs made doubles to be near and amongst us humans. Could that mean they make doubles of essential people and assist in ruling our world? Maybe so. Is this the work of a shadow government? If you have seen the movie Avatar, you might know how they make copies of people.

Just eight months later, on February 4, 2011, my youngest brother Brian told me he had a dream about me where he saw two of me simultaneously. I rarely ever talked to my youngest brother about my travels. He does not like to speak about such things as ETs, he's more interested in things like King Kong movies. But he is a special brother who has intuitive powers and a great memory. He told me he woke up scared and very confused about what he dreamt. Did my double enter my brother's dream? I hope my double is not a Doppelgänger. In folklore, if you meet your Doppelgänger twin, that is the day you die. I did not tell my brother anything about my experiences with doubles. I was afraid he would have more dreams.

14

TAOS HUM

The Taos HUM is a very low-frequency sound around 20 Hertz and lower. The human ear can only pick up low sounds *over* 20 hertz normally. I got the HUM on February 4, 2011; it struck me in the middle of the night. At first, I did not pay much attention to the low sound. It sounded like a diesel engine idling at a distance. The next day was when it seemed to bother me more. I looked up the Taos HUM on the internet and found The HUM Forum group. Various people wrote about their HUM dilemma and how it has affected their lives. I found a friend on the forum that is a scientist from the southwest and worked on electronic devices to detect the HUM. He had worked with the military as an engineer and gave me great information about the HUM, saying it was an ELF low frequency of 20 hertz or lower. He said the human ear should not be able to hear this ELF low frequency. But some people hear the HUM all over the world. A tiny percentage of humans hear the HUM, maybe less than five percent.

As I spoke to my scientist friend and also heard from others who have the HUM, it became clear that it was a vibration, not a sound. My research of this HUM frequency that I was afflicted with progressed, and I found no cure for the HUM. Once you have it, you don't lose the HUM. Since scientists cannot explain where the HUM comes from, there is not be a cure. I received a lot of information on the HUM, and it is a problematic anomaly to explain.

The Hum has been researched by city governments and federal governments to figure out what the HUM is. Even to this date, 2022, there is no explanation for the HUM. The HUM first started in Taos, New Mexico, in the early 1980s. People in that area seemed to acknowledge the HUM first. After that, it seemed to grow worldwide. Research continues by many scientists and engineers in order to solve the HUM source. You might be able to decrease the HUM's effect in your ears if you have white noise in the background like a fan. After ten years of having the HUM, I have learned to live with the inconvenience of the HUM. Others have a terrible time getting used to this HUM. Since it is a vibratory frequency, you would assume it would come from the ground. But it seems to come from the background and around your whole body.

There have been suggested possible sources of the HUM. Navy deep-sea sonic radar operations. Industrial complexes and their factory machinery humming. Exploration of the north and south poles utilizing high-tech apparatuses. The earth's natural humming frequency is an excellent possible source. Some scientists think it is flowing gas lines making the HUM underground. Another secret project, the HAARP atmospheric manipulation complexes using electrical and magnetic waves to alter the weather, also sounds like a good source.

In this author's opinion, I would have to blame extraterrestrial involvement in producing the HUM for their communication with each other. In February 2011, I had many UFO and ET experiences that could have given me the HUM. Could my implants cause me to get the HUM? Usually, I wait for other facts to drop before saying this ET conclusion. But one incident in particular made me think ET had something to do with this HUM. On March 17, 2011, when Hiroko (the humanoid ET with her sons) visited my house in Godfrey, Illinois, my cousin and I were sitting on my front porch in the early afternoon enjoying the nice weather. This incident bothered both of us, especially my cousin, since this was his first ET encounter. (You can read about this experience in an earlier chapter in this book.)

The day after the Hiroko visit, my cousin called me and said he had the darndest thing happen to him last night. He told me that he heard a low idling truck in the neighborhood but could not find it at 3 AM. He said it kept him awake, and he could not sleep all night. He asked me whether I know what it is that is humming. This was his comment:

"Was it those ETs from the other day that is making this sound"?

"It might be those ETs that caused you to hear the HUM." I responded.

"What the hell is the HUM?"

I then explained to him what it was and that yes, I think the ETs did this to him and I. It dawned on me that this was a strong possibility that when the ETs implant you, you can start having the HUM. I never heard any claim by others that ETs create the HUM. I think my cousin and I were in the right place and time to synchronize the source of the HUM with our meeting with ETs. Now I have a starting point for my source of the HUM. Since most people don't believe in ETs, that source will not be accepted by the general public.

My scientist friend said the people that hear the HUM might be chosen to hear it. Are the ETs choosing people for something? Is the HUM a tracking system for the ETs? Or is it a control frequency to gain access to our subconscious? Difficult for me to say because I had UFO/ET experiences before my HUM started.

High pitch sound in the left ear

About a year ago, I started getting a high pitch sound in my left ear above the already existing tinnitus pitch. Yes, we all have some tinnitus at some level due to health or damaged ears. My higher pitch starts when I touch my tongue on both of my two front teeth. Nowhere else causes this sound when I move my tongue around my mouth. I have no ear damage or problems with that left ear. Not saying I blame ETs for this problem, but it goes to reason that my abductions and my visits from ETs in my house last year could have placed an implant in my ear. What makes this more unusual is that I have seen three doctors since last year about this unique problem and none of them can figure this problem out and have never heard of this condition. You get used to strange things after a while dealing with ET experiences, as I have throughout life. This story is just a mention of a small issue, and there is no confirmation of what the problem is.

15

HYPNOSIS, SPIRITUAL GUIDE, PSYCHIC

Believe it or not, I am not a firm believer in psychics, but sometimes they make a good find in what you are looking for. I still believe that a natural lucid dream can regress your subconscious much better in a deep sleep. Hypnosis might inadvertently plant a seed in your thoughts that might give you false feedback of your regressed memory. Just the very nature of setting up the hypnotic session has you are prepared to tell the hypnotherapist about a UFO event. The most impressive reading I ever had was from a spiritualist in 2010. Native American Guides are summoned and they gave her the answers I was looking for. She was from Springfield, Illinois, and very nice and highly trusted. The following are my experiences with these three mediums.

The Psychic

I visited a well-established psychic in Sedona, Arizona, near the valley going to Cathedral Rock. When I first walked into her office, she looked at me then looked out her window. I greeted her, and she turned to me. For privacy purposes, I refer to her as "C" for now.

"It's Dave, right?" She asked.

"Yes, I'm here for my appointment." I said.

She remained looking out the window.

"Why are you looking at my car?" I asked.

"Dave, I saw a dark figure following you into the building."

"What do you mean?"

"You've had terrible experiences with ETs, right?" She turned her attention to me.

"Yes, I have but they don't follow people like that, do they?"

"They will. They like to monitor your activities." "C" said, "it could be your Angel protecting you also. Let's hope that is what it is. You have strong energy around you." Her eyes were powerful and piercing eyes.

"Dave, I think you already know the answers to your questions about your experiences with ETs. So, how can I help you?"

I imparted to her that I wanted to verify my thoughts about my experiences with UFOs/ETs. So, we talked for almost two hours, but it turned out to be a back and forth reading. She was reading me, and in retur, I would tell her about her life.

The psychic session scared me with "C" telling me that I was for real, and I have energy from my encounters that stays with me. It was reassuring to hear this from her and scary that people like her would notice my aura colors. "C" was slightly nervous during the session because of the dark shadowy figure she saw from the starting of our meeting. I told her that I tried to get an appointment for a psychic reading from another shop in town. But then the lady making my appointment looked like she feared me. I asked the owner why she acted so nervously around me. The owner said that I have a strong presence of energy around me, and she saw it as I came in the door. So "C" agreed that she noticed it too, but a psychic should not fear people so much as not to want to schedule a session. We had a couple of rewarding hours together, and I gave her a tip on top of her fee for answering my queries.

Hypnosis

I made an appointment to see a hypnotist forty minutes away from my home, who I'll call "L" for privacy purposes. This was in 2011 in a town in Illinois south of me. She was an experienced hypnotherapist with years of hypnotizing experience. She had many clients with ET experiences. So, I thought, *alright, I will give this a try*. When I got to her office, she told me to lay on the couch and relax. "L" asked me a few background questions and a little about my experiences. This is where I think it is wrong to plant the seed of ETs before the session. I told her about my latest events, starting with the large triangle craft I saw. She then said count backward from ten to one. As I counted, the HUM started getting very loud in my head, and I could not relax. She asked me a couple of questions about when my experiences happened. I kept being distracted by the HUM, the low diesel engine idling humming. I looked over at "L," and she was in a trance. I was wide awake and trying to talk to her. I called out her name three times, but she did not responding to me. I walked over to her desk and called her name out three more times. She finally came out of the trance and looked at me shocked and disoriented. She was not asleep, she had zoned out of consciousness.

When "L" lifted her head, she loudly said, "My God, those are rapture pick-up ships," meaning the large triangle UFO. She apologized for going into the trance state.

"I guess I was supposed to go into a trance, but I couldn't." I said. It seemed the hypnosis backfired on her. Instead of her putting me under hypnosis, she went under. She kept apologizing to me.

"That's alright. I will pay your fee and come back someday soon." I tried to ease her regret. She did not want the money because of the failed attempt to put me under but I gave the money to her anyway. I never made plans for another hypnosis session because it doesn't work for me. My question was, how come I was blocked from the hypnotic trance. Were there powers controlling my subconscious by bringing the HUM into full strength and loud? "L's" last words, before I left, were I should form a committee to write books and teach people about this rapture possibility. She then told me I would see Hiroko, the ET, again soon. She was right about that meeting.

Spiritualism

I was referred to this spiritualist by a ghost hunter and author, Larry, in Springfield, Illinois. He said she was the best he ever went to and that “C” was good at predicting one’s future through Indian guides. She was part Native American Indian, and her contacts with her guides turned real. I drove up a rocky road to her house, and it was like being in the country, but it was actually off a city street. I passed by a small pond, and as I was driving past it, I saw at least two hundred dragonflies fly across my car hood. My stomach buzzed from the synchronicity of seeing this many dragonflies on the way to a spiritualist’s house. She lived in a small half log and half pine siding house like a real country home. I walked inside and introduced myself.

“Hi, C. This is Dave.”

“I know.” She said with a smile. She had a shop full of artwork and Indian pottery and jewelry—a kind of Native American Indian style.

“C,” asked me to sit down at the desk. She started by lowering her head and meditating quietly.

She raised her head after a moment, “You have a bad back.”

"Alright, I would give that to you because I might have been bent over a little.” I responded, a bit dismissively. “I don’t not trust psychics very much.”

She looked at me a little irritated, “I am not a psychic, Dave. I am a spiritual reader with help from my guides.”

“OK, sorry about that.”

“You are planning on traveling soon.” She moved on from my skeptism.

“How did you know that?” This shocked me, I was planning a trip in two weeks time.

“The guides told me,” She responded.

"Yes, I am going out west for a trip and seeing some friends."

It was at that moment C noted that on October 4, 2010, I would meet my first ET in person. I told her I would be in Sedona, Arizona, on that date. She went back into meditation and then told me I would have car damage on the trip but would finish my trip.

"How bad of an accident will I have?" I asked her. She went quiet.

"My guides would not tell me about an accident. But the directions said it would be fine."

September 15, 2010 was the date that she gave me this information, long before October 4th.

Continuing the spiritualist remarks, "There is an alien implant in your right shoulder." Her last comment was that a blonde woman was looking for me. I thought deeply and tried to absorb what "C" told me during this session.

As we were parting, she said, "As I told you, I am not a psychic. My guides are right most of the time." Everything she told me came true; the car had hail damage; I met Hiroko, the ET, on October 4th. My right shoulder has electrical signals it gives off, meaning there is an implant, as she said. The blonde woman? I have seen so many strange people that I have no doubt I had met that woman already.

16

ABDUCTIONS THAT I AM CONSCIOUSLY AWARE HAPPENED

I had several of these bed-side ET DNA and semen collections. The first I remember was in 1995, and then in 2008, another collection of semen procedures was performed by ET. This happened around 2 AM early in the morning. I woke up from someone or something moving my right leg around. They were positioning my right leg where the knee was sticking up. I saw a brownish-colored hose about an inch diameter placed between my legs towards my groin. I looked up and saw a friend's face working the hose. When I saw my friend, I fell back off to sleep or was put to sleep by ETs. ETs mask their faces as somebody you know so you would not be so alarmed. They can delve into your subconscious and retrieve this information very quickly. They have mimicked sounds of voices and faces of humans, you know. This event foreshadowed the future of these visitations. UFOlogists have researched abductions with the help of a lot of prestigious academic people. They found that ETs can do bedroom lab work on humans just by putting them to sleep and sometimes people do not remember anything. Secondly, ETs can take your spirit and consciousness like an avatar for travel with them for lab work. This means you are physically in your body in bed, but they can quickly send your essence, spirit, and consciousness out of your body and back in. Lastly, ETs take your whole body temporarily, and you have missing time, and you might even have witnesses to your abduction. Whichever way the ETs abduct a person, they erase a large part of your memory with a bright light or use magnetic waves with a device about ten inches long and eight inches wide. Some abductees remember nothing and only feel a little tired in the morning. Researchers say around fifty percent of people abducted don't remember a thing.

First Electrical Shock

Starting on February 4, 2010, I felt an electric shock to my right index finger. I fell asleep and heard this loud popping that sounded like an electrical wire short pop. Before the popping sound, I heard static electricity for a brief time and then I felt the tip of my finger hurting and burning. I thought, due to the popping sound, that I had lost my finger. Jumping up, I turned on the bedroom light and examined my finger. My index finger was delicate, with no burn or damage from the popping sound. It was still burning and sore for a while. I checked all around where my hand could have touched an electrical source. My clock was battery-operated, and the lamp was far away from my right hand. I was lying a distance from the nightstand, so I knew it was not an electrical shock from my nightstand.

That day I had the flu, and I could not breathe very well. My chest was congested with a bronchitis condition that has plagued me since birth. I set my clock for an early morning visit to my doctor. I thought maybe I had pneumonia. When I got to my doctor's office the following day, she gave me a physical with a concentration of the lungs. I chose not to tell the doctor about the electrical shock I got the night before because doctors often don't get involved with the strange happenings. The doctor said my lungs sound alright, but they wanted to take an x-ray to ensure that my breathing difficulty isn't pneumonia. The test came back negative for a lung problem. She gave me a Z pack and sent me home. The one thought that came to my mind was that this was an angel healed my lungs that night. But as we continue my experiences, you will find out differently. This was not a random electrical problem. Strange energies caused this shock on my finger.

Lucid Dream with ET Physical Contact Abduction

2010 was the year that ET and their abductions intensified their presence and my experiences increased. Lucid dreams have occurred quite frequently for me since 2008. Not all of them are connected with ETs, so I don't mention them here. As far as dreams are concerned, I must have a solid connection to a physical ET event to confirm the strangeness. My lucid dreams all have a meaning from a tangible source. I won't discuss questionable dreams in this book.

I dreamt of meeting a strange long dark-haired woman in this lucid dream. Usually, babies, women, and sometimes romantic interludes occur in these dreams. This lucid dream went into physical contact with ET. It started with me hearing static electricity crackling in the hallway. I was half-awake when these strange physical events occurred. Hands were brushing my body parts, nothing sexual, just legs and chest were touched. I felt someone or something touching my feet like they were examining them. I then felt a strong pull-down of my right foot with fingers on top of my foot and underneath my toes. From what I felt, they were fingertips bending my foot. Whatever it was, an ET or else, it yanked hard on my foot, waking me up with pain in the right foot. This is the first time I felt pain from an ET experience.

There were marks all over my body. I took pictures of most of what I could see. What I failed to do was to take photos of the blood droplets on my bedsheets. There were scars on my left leg that I could not figure out. I took pictures of the wounds. It seemed like a practice that the entities pull down on my feet to wake me up. Maybe they are humane about abductions. Do they want to make sure you are still alive? After my wake-up, I heard what sounded like humans whistling in other rooms of the house. This often happens, hearing whistle sounds during and after an abduction.

Most Intense Electrical Shock Abduction

On July 17, 2011, at around 4 PM, I felt tired working on my computer, so I took a rest period for my backaches. Sometimes the ETs will hit you with magnetic energy to make you tired to abduct you easily. There was something small and thin next to me in bed and I could feel some weight where it was laying, sinking the mattress somewhat. I was lying on my left side with my left elbow leaning on the mattress, cupping my chin in the palm of my hand. Whatever this small object was, it shocked me until I was paralyzed. The jolt of static electrical energy hit my right shoulder and stopped me from moving around. I tried moving again, forcing my shoulder first, then the energy hit me again in the right shoulder. My right shoulder coincidently is where the spiritualist told me there was an implant. After the second large dose of energy, I was completely immobilized at that time. I could only move my fingertips of the left hand and roll my eyes a little. I was looking out of my bedroom door, and could see that the sun was very bright, so I was aware this was a daytime abduction.

I felt a presence in the room behind me, standing next to my bed. I tried to turn to look but could not move. I have had sleep paralysis before a couple of times, but this was not even close to sleep paralysis. I heard a familiar voice coming from the hallway near the second bathroom. It was my sister's voice.

"Come on, Dave, you can do it," She was telling me.

"Do what, Sissy?" I asked. Sissy was my sister who passed away four years earlier. That is alarmed me. How could this be my sister's voice? She repeated it.

"Come on, Dave, you can do it."

This time she was pounding on the wall in the next room over. Fear started settling in after that. I think she was trying to warn me about something. I called out to her, "Come to the doorway where I can see you."

"I can't," She said.

"Why can't you, Sissy?"

"I just can't come to the door," she said, "Come on, Dave, just do it." Then she said, "What are you doing?"

Again, I told her, "Come to the doorway."

Her last words were, "I can't." After that, her voice stopped, and it went quiet except for the crackling going on behind me that I could not see. I think she was trying to tell me to get away from the ETs. My sister must have come through a portal that the ETs opened. Or the ETs were mimicking her voice to get through to me and be in total control.

My left arm was still leaning up against the headboard with my left hand in a slightly open position. I felt very much awake and conscious of what was happening around me. *This is no sleep paralysis*, I thought to myself. I also was considering my sister's voice was coming from another dimension. Either way, the ETs open the portal. What happened next really got me thinking. In my left hand, something dropped a baby's tiny hand into my left hand. I could move my fingertips. So, I started pulling down on the little fingers and pulled on the little palm of the baby. The baby felt like it was just born recently because of the size of the baby's hand and fingers. It was a human or a hybrid child. Its hand was soft and smooth. It was genuine. Whoever held the baby upside down over the headboard must have been tall. It appeared to be the baby's right hand I was feeling. The entity was leaning over me and dangling the baby's hand into my left hand's fingertips. The ET pulled the baby's hand back up from my hand, and it was gone. Still, while all this was going on, I was thinking, "*Was this my hybrid baby that could have been conceived by a semen sample in Sedona nine months earlier?*" After that, I kept staring out the sunlit door and trying to talk to whatever was controlling me. By asking the ETs, "what do you want, why are you doing this to me? Who was that baby?"

It seemed like what was behind me kept weakening me more the longer this went on. I kept hearing the static electricity crackling, and it was terrifying. I felt that this was my baby hybrid born with my DNA from the Sedona semen collection. I thought back to Hiroko, who said she needed a baby. I still could not move anything on my body except my eyes and fingertips. These thoughts about the baby came from my gut, deep, real feelings. I felt a heavy solid object near my hip area in the bed. The bed mattress was weighed down more, and I could feel it. I was wildly shaken up at that time when the solid body moved closer to me in bed. I started saying the Lord's Prayer out loud verbally. In sleep paralysis, you can only mumble words, but I could talk very well. My right shoulder kept hurting from the constant electrical energy being put on it. That is when I yelled out loud, "God help me." As soon as I said that it was over, everything was gone.

After this abduction, I felt that my muscles were sore, I was exhausted and shaking. Sit up in bed and saw the whole bed was in disarray with sheets and blanket nearly off the bed. I had also noticed a slight pounding on the mattress during this episode. I spoke to Dr. David Jacobs at an Arkansas UFO Convention and told him about this experience. In response, he chuckled.

"You don't believe me?" I asked, incredulous.

"No, your abduction ended, and the ETs brought you back," He said, "This happens to abductees because of all the confusion and fear associated with abduction. The electrical energy was bringing you back to your bed."

I maintained a charge in my DNA from all the electrical energy I was exposed to from three electrically charged events by ET. That is why I shock my wife a lot by touching her. My cell phone won't work for me sometimes. Hospital testing equipment does not get good readings because of the extra electricity in my body.

Energy Rope wrapped Abduction

It seems that ETs' active hours are between 3 AM and 5 AM to work on human consciousness and DNA. Maybe because they are usually deep in sleep and quickly put us, humans, into a deeper subconscious mode.

On September 2, 2011, before 4 AM, it felt like a rope was wrapped around my whole body. I woke up from my sleep and felt this energy wrapping around me. I could hardly move being tied up in bed. I felt a strong tingling feeling all over my body, like energy shooting through the rope. I could see that it was not a physical rope, just transparent energy. My body felt warm, and my pulse rate increased. A minute later, I slipped into a lucid dream like I was transported somewhere.

I ended up seated with a group of soldiers (military people) I did not know. I saw some old friends from my past jobs sitting around a table. Again, my beliefs are that ETs mask people and make them look like people you know to keep you calm. I have been with the ETs mimicking and masking as people I know. And I knew ETs were manipulating this lucid dream. I ended up in Antarctica, where people were sunbathing. There were little mean animals taking peoples' clothing while they sunbathed. The little animals were the size of the domesticated cat. Before all the recent discoveries about Antarctica, this dream was shown as a futuristic phenomenon. This lucid dream seemed scripted like I was on a guided tour of Antarctica. I found myself romancing a woman that was very tall and attractive. In my past abductions, she looked like an ET, a tall white ET about seven feet tall.

As my dream of Antarctica progressed, I saw this same tall white female with no hair, big green eyes, and a perfect body like most tall whites have. She got up from sunbathing with her other friends and left abruptly. It did not seem like I was on earth, maybe below Antarctica, another warm underworld. My thoughts were that the tall whites were monitoring me throughout my life. The rope around me meant it was a DNA chain. This is not the first encounter with these tall whites. I keep telling people that I can't make this stuff up. Not a writer or science fiction enthusiast, so where do these ideas come from?

Another Static Electrical Abduction

I was sick most of the day on September 6, 2011, had a fever, and felt like my whole body was burning hot. It was around 9:30 PM, and I went to bed because I felt terrible. I was very much awake and conscious of my surroundings. Then I heard a familiar sound of the static electrical energy next to my bedside and I became partially paralyzed and could not move much. I raised my right arm and pushed the power away from me, thinking, *not this time.* It felt like I was pushing back on a lot of weight and force, but I kept pushing hard, and I was winning the pushback. It was an electrical force I was going against, not weight, although it felt like it.

I pointed at the area where the static electrical sounds were coming from and said, "No, not this time." I jumped out of bed as quickly as I could. I then distanced myself from the energy area of the bedroom. I was shaking and felt like I was buzzing all over. I reminded myself they were done with me, and I did not stop the abduction. It would seem these are the same ETs abducting me because of their mode of operation with the electrical charges. I was getting weary of these intrusions in my life by ET and wondering why they couldn't stop messing with me.

Put my Arm through a Steel Door

On November 11, 2011, (11/11/11), this good synchronicity of numbers helped me bring up a solid lucid regressed dream.

At around 5 AM, I had a regressed lucid dream that I can say is real. I think the ETs wanted me to have knowledge of this abduction event to show how they can pass through walls. ETs walked me through my house to the living room from the bedroom. At the beginning, I felt warm with a slight tingling sensation. When I arrived in my living room, I could tell there were several entities behind me telepathically communicating with me. I started feeling like I was thin and light as a feather when approaching my living room door. I never saw these ETs and presume they must have been invisibly cloaked. As they kept telling me telepathically to go through the door, I got worried I would hurt myself. I did not want to bump my head into the steel-insulated door. So, I reached out with my right arm towards the door, bracing for impact.

I looked back again to see If I could see the ETs but nobody behind me.

"Is anybody watching this door walkthrough?" I said out loud. I always wanted a camera to record my thoughts while going through these experiences, but you never have a camera when you need it because you never know when ET shows up. And even if you had a camera, the ETs would disable it or run the batteries down. To my surprise, my arm went through the steel door up to my right elbow.

"Can anybody get a picture of my arm in the metal door?" I called out. You can see I was becoming hysterical and scared, talking out of my head. I guess I did not have control of my mind, the ETs controlled it.

The longer my arm was through the steel door, the more my arm started burning - more and more. I felt weak, nauseous, confused; my body felt like it was spinning out of control, my heart rate was high, and fear rapidly crept in as I decided I needed to finish going through the door. I was afraid that my arm would burn up if I did not finish going through the door. There was no memory of what happened after getting my whole body to my front porch and outside. I could strongly guess that I was a tractor beamed up to a UFO craft. One of my other regressed dreams must have finished my abduction experience from this event. It is difficult to match the appropriate regressed dream to the actual abduction if you have had several as I have.

I got up a couple of hours or so later and took a look at my arm. It was red, as though lightly sunburn. My body still felt hot after the incident of walking through the door. I wrote my scientist friend and asked him what happens to a body if it walks through metal doors. He requested I write to him and list my symptoms during the abduction. He told me not to tell him anything else beyond this and let him write his opinion down. I wrote him a long email listing all my side effects from walking through the door. After he responded to the symptoms, I wrote him what I listed above in this experience. He wrote back, explaining this was not a dream, this had happened. "J," said that to go through matter of any kind, your cells must speed up with frequencies driving the body's denseness to be porous enough to work through other molecules like the door. ETs do this with high frequencies to go through solid mass. There is a magnetic energy component to this frequency becoming faster. A couple days later, I was still feeling uneasy and still felt the burning sensation. My body's atoms were sped up, that is why I was weak and nauseous. This scientist was a professional and knew a lot about these energy frequency manipulations. I could have simply been a copy like a holographic avatar of myself. We are not sure how we travel onboard ETs ships when abducted – food for thought. ETs being possibly millions of years ahead of us, anything is possible with their technology.

ETs Strumming my Guitar

It was January 15, 2012; I woke up at 2:30 am in bed half-paralyzed like the other abductions I am familiar with in the past. I felt an entity or something in the bedroom with me. I could not see my visitors because these ETs often cloaked with invisibility, as they were now. I heard my guitar being strummed in the other room.

"What the hell?" I said to myself. I hadn't heard anything or entity playing my guitar before. It got spooky from that point on. They just made a noise with the guitar, there was no real music. *ETs don't know how to play guitar*, I thought. After that, my fan switched to high, doubling the noise. At the same time, my bed was being pushed down by something with weight. I felt something grab my right foot and felt fingertips under my toes. Then, as usual, this entity yanked down on my foot, hurting it, and I jumped. I never saw anybody in the room when I looked around. Especially in the daytime, I would be unable to see the ETs. Yes, this same abduction or ET visit sounds familiar because this sequence of ET seems their standard procedure.

I lay in bed for several minutes, still unable to move my body. I could only roll my eyes. I felt that the visitors were trying to send me a message of some kind. I wondered why they wanted to aggravate me and try to scare me for some reason. The ETs finally left, and I was able to move again. I went around the house praying and trying to get rid of this negative visitation, as during the last few minutes of these ETs trying to scare me, I felt negative energy in the bedroom.

Vibrating Electrical Pulses in my Bedroom

In May of 2012, while I was in bed around 3:45 AM, I heard vibrating pulses in my bedroom, and it woke me up from sleep. Then the electrical energy hit my whole body. Right after that, my body was paralyzed. I could move around, but I couldn't move at all. Just like a year or more ago, the crackling sound of static electricity was deafening. I panicked and started reaching for objects to help me get out of bed; I tried reaching for my cell phone and clock. I wanted to call my family because I thought I had a heart attack. Going for the clock did not make sense to me later because why did I need to know the time? After several ET abduction shocks, I was concerned about my heart and how these electrical pulses would affect my body.

It seemed my mind and thoughts were turned off by the second big jolt of electrical energy. I felt like I passed out several times during these initial electrical energy charges. I tried to see the time on the clock next to my bed, but my eyes were blurry. Finally, I saw that it was 4:12 AM. There were no stroke symptoms like indigestion, no headache, no fast pulse, no sweats, and my breathing was fine. My bedroom was 68 degrees, so no hot flashes. After confirming the vitals of my body, I went back to sleep.

Almost an hour after I fell asleep, I had a very lucid dream (regression) that I ended up in a large storeroom dimly lit with lights. First, I saw a woman that looked human with a white gown dress that was white and almost see-through. She was beautiful and looked like the last tall white ET woman I saw over the last two years. She had pale skin and was very tall, around six foot seven inches in height. She had no hair, but it did not detract from her attractiveness. I had to look up at her, she was so much taller than me. I tried to speak to her, but she just looked at me with large blue eyes, sending telepathic thoughts at me. She led me around on the ship, and I saw a cluttered supply room filled with crates that were metal. The humanoid woman walked away quickly because someone told her to leave me in the supply room. I was then told to go to this other room to meet someone. The ship was darker than my regular visits on ET craft. I walked into this smaller darkened room that had a large bed made in a curved shape.

In this large bed was a large reptilian lying down. The reptilian looked like a large cobra that seemed to oversee the rest of them. They were all dark green, and it was hard to make out details because of the darkness within the room. Several smaller reptilian beings were surrounding the big reptilian. Then a large reptilian came in the room and bent down and kissed the leader's forehead. Since I am afraid of snakes, this was very scary to me being in a room with five or six of these entities. Since I saw a small reptilian in my bedroom once, I knew what I saw on this ship. They had long fingers with long fingernails, large arms and enormous chests. The smaller ones were not as scary as these two large reptilians. The large reptilian looked at me and telepathically told me to follow him. I went with him, and he showed me a room of electronic apparatuses. They could have been weapons, but I really could not make these objects out because of the very dim lighting. He put a small brown ring object on my middle finger and then shined a bright light on it. It shrunk and got very tight, causing me pain and I tried to remove it. When he saw my reaction to the pain, he shined a light back on the ring, and it loosened up. This ring and controls were likely to keep track of me on the ship. It must have been a large ship, I did not see the whole thing. I noticed that the reptilians had their dark lenses off, and I could see the whites of their eyes. The color of their irises was a green slit, like typical reptile. Being dark on the craft, they did not use lenses. After that, I only remember being back in bed. I wondered why one of the ETs was a tall white woman ET with a ship full of reptilians. Since she obeyed her supervisor and left quickly, this told me she was maybe enslaved.

17

IMPLANTS

1963 FLYING SAUCER IMPLANT

The first implant I received was in 1963 The when my best friend and I saw our first flying saucer. (You can read this story at the front of the book in Chapter Two.) I did not know it had been implanted until a couple of weeks after our sighting. This is when I felt something like a bump in my left testicle and thought it was not normal. Upon closer inspection, I saw a thin red line about an inch long that seemed to be a shallow cut, what we would call today a laser cut. Being only 14 years of age, I figured out it had to be from the flying saucer we saw.

Not only did we see the craft, but I also had a regressed dream that showed me we both were onboard the alien craft together. I started pushing the lump in my teste towards the thin red line, and I knew it was put in me from that red line. I kept going, it hurt only a little; there was no blood when I finally pushed out the implant.

I finally worked the lump out of my left testicle, and it looked like an Advil tablet and was about the same size. The implant was a white ash color while I held it in my hand. The longer I had it out in the open air; the implant started brown. I took it to my mother, and showed her.

"What is that thing?" she asked.

"It came from my testicle area." I responded.

"I think its an ingrown hair or a blackhead."

"No, Mom, there was a thin red line cut for this thing to be put in my teste. I pushed it through the red line, and it came right out."

My Mother looked puzzled and said, "throw it away."

"Alright, but it is strange, don't you think, mom?" I said. She responded by telling me to go and play. Back in the 60s, we knew very little about ETs and UFOs. They were called flying saucers. My mom protected me from becoming too scared because she warned us not to approach a flying saucer. In later years, I found out she had seen flying saucers several times but had no pictures.

Second Implant in 2011

My second implant was found in February 2011. The implant had been there long before I found it in my left leg muscle. So, I don't know when I was implanted with it. I guess it might have been put in my leg during my visit to Sedona, Arizona, with the meeting of Hiroko (see Hiroko story). My leg had an itch on the inside of my left calve muscle. I kept scratching the leg and eventually noticed a little red hole like the red line I found on my left teste. I got a tissue, and when I scratched the round red hole hard enough, a blood bubble came out. I took my cotton tissue and soaked the blood up. When I lifted the tissue away from my leg, I saw a small dark charcoal color solid object in the blood. I took out the tangible thing and looked at it through my small microscope. The implant was 3/8" inch long and 5/16" inch wide. After looking at it, the implant object looked like it had synapsis or brain cells that were like tiny octopuses. The lump of dark was alive, and it changed shapes as it went along in time. I put it in a plastic bag to preserve it and then took it to a camera specialist to take microscopic pictures. He told me it was not hair follicles and did not know what it was.

I started taking pictures myself after the camera specialist spent a lot of time on the implant. His pictures were of bad quality. I took photos of the implant with my Sony Cam through the microscope lens. I wish I had known I could take microscopic pictures before giving it to the camera specialist. I put the implanted sample in the refrigerator to keep it longer.

I took the implant to a UFO group I belonged to with my small microscope and let the group of twenty people look at the implant through the microscope. My friend and biologist supervisor at St. Louis University looked closely at the implanted sample. She said she had never seen anything like this in all her career of 40 years. After that showing, I took it home and took many pictures of this implant. I will include photos of the implant in this book. It took about one month for the implant to dissolve totally in the plastic bag. I took pictures of it during its deterioration. ETs make mostly biological implants that dissolve when exposed to oxygen to hide any evidence of implant. The metal implants are quite different and will last much longer. The ETs also put decoy implants in you to throw you off the actual implants – like a smoke screen. Maybe the actual implant is in my right shoulder, as the spiritualist told me.

Left Thumb Anomaly – Implant

I noticed a lump in my left thumb eight years ago. It is movable and feels hard and solid under the skin. I had x-rays taken of the hand in 2016 because it hurt just a little when I pressed on the lump. It did not give me much discomfort, so I let it go and lived with it. I can move the bump around under the skin. The doctor who took the x-rays said it existed and it shows up white on the underside joint of the left thumb in the x-ray.

The doctor went on to say if it caused me pain, he could remove the lump. I told him I would hold off on that surgery unless it begins hurts. I was told through other implant research that most implants are placed on the left side of the body. They can go unnoticed for years. The ETs are experts in this field of implants, and I think our government has back-engineered their work with implants.

Right Thumb Small Red Hole with Small lump

I had another implant that I noticed just a year ago in 2020; it too had a small red hole just above the nail quick. About three-eighths of an inch away from a round hole, there was a small object the size of a BB and hard to the touch. It would hurt when pressed on. I could move it a little, but it got sore with movement. It felt to be a one-eighth inch in diameter object. The red hole above the thumbnail lasted long and never healed for about a year.

As of January 29, 2021, it is gone entirely and must have dissolved into my body and probably was intended that way. It reminds me of the left thumb hard lump at the thumb joint. Why would a hard object be in the thumbnail area and a red hole near the thing? It seems these thin red lines and red holes have something in common. They are purposely put there for implant purposes by ET.

TSA Magnetic/Frequency Security Screening Exposing Implants

I had some trouble with the Airport TSA screenings on January 12, 2015 at the Fairbanks, Alaska airport, beginning my trip to the Philippines with my wife. My wife and I both went through screenings together with TSA. Our suitcases were OK, and the magnetometer wand of the body was alright also. When I got to the circular rotating magnetic and frequency testing equipment, I put my arms in the air as required. I was stopped by an agent when I exited the test platform. My wife said, "come on, Baby, let's go." But the TSA agent said I was not going anywhere.

"Why am I being stopped?" I asked the agent.

"You see that human silhouette on the side of the machine." He pointed to it.

"Yes."

"It has five orange circles on your body scan from your right shoulder to your stomach."

"What do those circles mean?"

"I don't know, but it tells me we need to find out more about those spots."

"You don't know what they are?" I was confused.

"No, I don't." He responded. I looked at the orange circles.

"Am I in trouble now?" I asked. The agent seemed very nervous and told me to step aside for more testing. They checked my pockets and rubbed my hands and arms with a cotton pad. They even tested me again with the magnetic wand. They found no gun powder or anything on me that would make the orange circles on the silhouette to show warnings. After clearing me, they gave me a red card and told me to give it to the stewardess. I knew what that card meant; it meant *keep an eye on me.*

That was a tense few moments because I thought the agents would bump me off the flight. I did not want to tell them that I thought they were remnants from ET implants. TSA has no sense of humor. The right shoulder was the brightest orange circle on the silhouette, and I know what that indicated – implant.

San Francisco TSA Screening with Orange Circles on Human Silhouette – Again

I went through another tense few minutes at the San Francisco Airport TSA screening. One year after the Alaskan screening, I was being tested on the revolving magnetic, frequencies, and smell testing machine. I went through the same process. I started getting off the device, and the TSA agent grabbed my arm firmly.

I looked at him and said, "What's the problem, officer?" He pointed at the silhouette as the agent did a year prior. I saw the same five orange circles that I saw in Alaska. I told him this had happened before officer in Alaska and I asked him if he knew what the circles meant.

"No, I don't. I hadn't seen these circles like what is showing on the human silhouette before." He answered.

"What could they be?" I asked.

"I don't know, but you have to go over there for more testing."

This TSA agent also seemed nervous trying to figure out what the orange circles meant.

Two TSA agents took me aside and checked me all over, padding my body for weapons. They swabbed me and ran the magnetometer over my body. I thought I would not be so lucky this time because these officers were serious. They cleared me, and they called somebody in airport security. The same thing again, watch this guy. After this happening with the orange warning circles again within a year apart, I thought this was no fluke happening. I can only figure it had something to do with ET implants because my right shoulder was the brightest area in orange. And it was the same five circles from my shoulder to my stomach area. The second time this happens is apparent; these are anomalies from ET.

My car had an Implant from ET

After the humanoid ET Hiroko visited my Godfrey house on March 17, 2011, I noticed something about my car console area a couple of days later. I was visiting my brother Mick out in the country for a party with our families. When I got into my car to leave, I noticed that the middle console area was scorching hot against my right leg. This is the same leg operating the gas pedal, and I leaned against the carpeted console. The more I drove the car, the hotter the console got. After driving a while, I could not lean my leg against the console due to how hot it was.

I took my car home and measured the magnetic energy in the area where the heat was coming from with my tri-field meter. I considered that ambient electrical readings would be there, so I measured directly over the hot spot and made allowances for the difference in readings. The meter measured seven on the hundred scales in the magnetic EMF range. I smelled a hot vinyl smell emanating from the car's floor as I was taking readings. I took a temperature reading from the heat gun I had just purchased. The heat gun measured one hundred sixty to one hundred eighty degrees Fahrenheit. It seems the temperature changed in a concentric circle from the outside ring to the center of the circle being the hottest.

I took my car to my dealer service department in town the next day. The car was less than a year old at this time and should not have these problems. The shop manager told me that it is impossible, there was nothing under the console that can get that hot. The manager got his heat gun and measured the temperature.

After about a minute of testing the whole console area, he looked up, "I am getting one hundred eighty degrees. That is crazy, it should never be that hot."

He took the car into the shop right away because of the fire hazard it presented. He said he found nothing that would cause that kind of heat about an hour later and that they doubled the insulation, and the console should be better now. They told me to bring it back if it gets hot again. I asked the manager whether they put metal backing insulation under the console carpet.

"No, why? It won't work if it is not metal-backed insulation." He said The supervisor knew of my travels out west and ET and UFO studies. "Do you know something we don't?"

"Maybe," I said "but I wouldn't know for sure."

The supervisor told me I better be careful with those strange ETs. Later that evening, after driving for a while, I measured the console with my heat gun. It seemed to be in a five-inch circle shape, with the hottest part being in the middle of the bullseye. I got one hundred eighty degrees in the very center. Well, back to the dealer's shop the next day to tell them the plain insulation won't work. The manager asked me why the metal backing insulation would work better. I explained because it is heat that is radiating in circles. It is radiant heat, not direct heat to the console. He looked at me strangely and said he would call Detroit engineers and do what they say to do.

After he called the Detroit engineers, he said they didn't answer the problem. Then he said they would do what the customer asked and put the metal-backed insulation in the console. So, they went to Home Depot for the metal-backed insulation and put it in the car console. The manager asked me how I knew that information about eliminating the problem. The supervisor interjected, telling him he would not understand how Dave knew this method of solving the problem. I asked them to wait until tomorrow to see if the heat comes back after installing the metal-backed insulation. The next day everything was fine, with no heat coming from the console area so I called and told the manager the heat problem stopped.

"How did you know about the type of insulation it required?" He inquired.

"That is a long story, and you won't believe it anyway. Ask the supervisor; he knows some of my experiences." I responded, and hung up the phone.

There is no doubt many people walking around with implants in them that have not noticed them yet. Just like abductions, fifty percent don't know they were abducted. There are several reasons why I think a person gets implanted by ET. First, to track their subjects (us humans). Secondly, to change our frequencies for higher consciousness. Third, DNA manipulation of our bodies makes us more intelligent and more at peace. Look at our evolution; ETs have changed us into today's modern humans.

18

BODY FROZEN IN THE MIDDLE OF NIGHT

My freezing events started on August 13, 2016, at around 1 AM in bed. Before that, my wife said she was cold around 11 PM and shaking. She said she heard noises like knives scraping together or a metallic sound during her freezing event. This was near our bedroom where the noises happened. I have heard those sounds before that night. A metallic sound accompanies the cross-over when an entity comes through a portal. A dimensional barrier will create pop sounds or metallic sounds. The air conditioner was running, and it was 70 degrees in the bedroom that night, a typical hot summer night. We both had our blankets on, so we should not have been freezing.

I had my freezing event just two hours after my wife's cold event. I woke up freezing, and my body felt cold and dead. I felt my arms, and they were frozen. I got up and walked to the bathroom, shaking all the way. I sat down on the toilet and wondered what was happening to my body. I did not feel chest pains or any kind of body malfunction except for being frozen and weak. When I went back to bed, I shook the whole bed with how hard I was shivering. I covered up with blankets and, to my surprise, fell asleep rapidly. I figured I was exhausted and tired from what had just happened. It was no coincidence that we both felt like we were freezing. Something had come into our bedroom and drew our energy away from us. Of course, my thoughts were that the ETs were doing some experiments on us in our house. I have ghost-hunting friends who tell me they also get a freezing feeling when spirits jump them. This is similar to what we went through that night—taking our energy for some reason, maybe using our power for dimensional travel.

The second time the freezing event happened, I was alone and my wife was not present for this event. On August 16, 2017, a year almost to the date from the first freezing event, I woke up at 2:30 AM shaking badly again, shaking the whole bed and freezing. I did the same thing, felt my body, and felt very cold to the touch. I got up, went to the bathroom, and sat on the toilet, shaking vigorously. I went back to bed, covered up, and fell asleep immediately due to exhaustion. The room temperature was 70 degrees, and the air conditioner was working. I should have never gotten so cold with blankets on. My thoughts were *did the ETs pay us another visit and drain my energy again*? Before the freezing event, I had a lucid dream, this time proceeding the freezing episode. I found myself in a large room looking at a paper diagram with lines on it. Then I went towards a large hill in my dream and approached a large house or castle. After is when I felt the freezing of my body.

My third time of freezing in the middle of the night in bed, was on January 24, 2019, around 3 AM, while asleep. Some noise awakened me, and I opened my eyes but never saw anything in the bedroom. I was shaking all over and felt very cold. I touched my body, and it felt like I was dead because my whole body was very cold to the touch. I figured this was another freezing incident similar to the previous. So, this time did not scare me as much. I got out of bed and went to the bathroom to urinate. In each freezing episode, I immediately must urinate. Like other freezing incidents, the room was 70 degrees, and we had our blankets over us. I could not account for the freezing. I went back to bed shivering a lot and covered up again with blankets. Again, I fell off to sleep very quickly because I was tired due to whatever had happened to me. My routine doctor visit was just a few days later. I brought up the freezing episodes to my doctor. She is an excellent doctor and I thought she would know something about freezing bodies. She asked me, "were you just cold or freezing as you say?" I answered her by saying I was frozen like I was dead. I felt my body, and I was ice cold on my arms and legs – my total body was frozen. My doctor looked at my medical record and noted that I don't have any noticeable heart trouble, no diabetes, or natural health issues that would cause the freezing of your body. I asked her what these freezing incidents were because I have had freezing events now three times. She said, "I don't know." She told me to record these freezing episodes and call me if I had a medical issue.

The freezing of my body in bed did not stop, it happened the fourth time. On August 10, 2019, I had another freezing episode. Exact same conditions, my body felt frozen to the bone, and the room was 69 degrees, and I had a sheet and bedspread covering me and yet I was so cold that it was tough to move around. I was shaking the whole bed with my hard shivers. During these last three freezing episodes, my wife never woke up, and I wondered why. I went to the bathroom to urinate, as was routine during these icy attacks. I got back to bed, covered up, and went directly asleep due to feeling weak. All of these freezing episodes are very similar and repetitive, but I want to let you know there is a reason for me to tell you about all these freezing events. I felt a freezing ripple going up and down my whole body like being in waves and losing your body's energy will make you very cold and shaky. But what is taking my energy? The first thing that comes to mind is ETs.

I spoke to a second different doctor, and he asked me health questions—no heart trouble at present, no circulation problem, and no diabetes or blood abnormalities. Well, the doctor said he didn't know.

"It is odd to me," he said. He told me to take my temperature when I get these freezing episodes and to let him know if this problem gets worse.

These first four freezing events happened almost to the day, one year apart each time. This is the most revealing of these five events, how they happened nearly the same day every year. The exception is 2018, where there were no freezing episodes. But clearly, the ETs were late for some reason. The freezing attack that happened on January 24, 2019 was to make up for the summer of 2018 they missed. The freezing event was like all the rest of the freezing of the body experiences. I woke up feeling like I was freezing to death and went to the bathroom. I got back to bed and fell off to sleep fast. I also mentioned this to a doctor at my clinic about the freezing occurrences. This was a different doctor. He was the third doctor try to diagnose my freezing problem. The doctor looked at my medical record and said there was no medical problem that could have this freezing effect on my body. He said, "I don't know to be honest with you," —still no answers to this freezing dilemma.

This freezing problem did not stop. It happened again on September 2, 2021, the fifth freezing episode. Of course, the same thing happened room was 70 degrees; blankets were over us, and I shook the bed from my freezing shakes. I remember being so cold my arms felt like they would never come back to life. I did not feel any pain or heart issues. I went to the bathroom to urinate and shook the whole way. I went back to bed and fell off to sleep very fast due to exhaustion.

I talked to another different doctor about my freezing episodes. He went into my medical records and asked me some questions. The doctor said he had no idea what could be causing this condition. Like one other doctor said, he recommended taking my temperature during my freezing attacks. ETs have visited me a lot in the past, and I would be inclined to think they are doing this to me. If they are taking my consciousness, mind, and soul in an abduction, they would be taking my body's energy with it. That would leave my body cold and freezing. Maybe they have a way to freeze the body to keep it from biologically dying while the body's energy is gone. The only year that the freezing was missing was 2020. The reason for that was I had several ETs in my house from February to June of 2020, who I got pictures and films of three of.

19

APPORTS

AMBER AMULET MISSING FOR THREE DAYS

On February 17, 2011, I lost my Amber Amulet in my bedroom. The Amulet detached from my silver necklace one morning when I got up from sleeping. The eyelet that attached the Amulet to the necklace was not broken or bent, so I had a hard time figuring out how it got off the chain. It was a solid chain and would have never broken off unless purposely pulled on strongly. I looked everywhere for the Amulet under the bed, all over the floor, checked all drawers, and tore the bed apart looking for the Amulet and I could not locate it. The Amulet had been on my chain, and I was wearing it while I slept, and when I awoke it was missing.

The Amulet was gone for over two days. What makes this a strange incident is that somebody or something took it for two days. Secondly, while brushing my hair in front of the mirror, I felt something hard, and the brush caught on the lump. So, I slowly removed the lump in my hair that had my hair knotted up. When I got it out, I could not believe my eyes. The lump was the lost Amber Amulet that I did not see for two days. It fell on the floor while brushing my hair when I finally saw the Amulet. I was beside myself when I saw the Amulet. Where could it have been for two days, and why was it in my hair? I guessed that the humanoid ET Hiroko might have taken it. She liked the Amulet when I met her four months earlier. Apports come from several different sources, not necessarily ETs. There are dimensional theories that entities crossover the veil and take small articles or leave small pieces. Jewelry is the central piece of interest they like the most, it seems. Another theory is those invisible entities including, poltergeists, ETs, Big Foot, or invisible time travelers.

Pretty Agate Rock on Car Floor

This Apport came into being on April 11, 2011, and was found on the floorboard of my car. The day before, I cleaned the car floor and picked up a quarter in the exact place the rock was found so I knew it was not there. The day after cleaning, I saw the colorful small agate rock sitting where the coin was the day prior. The stone was five eights inches long by quarter-inch thick. I did not bring the colorful agate rock home from the out west trip. It was very mysterious how this rock showed up in the car. My car was locked so that nobody could get into the car and it was placed exactly where I picked up the quarter, so they put things where you will see them. Apports are souvenirs and a gift from out of another dimension or ET entity.

First Mysterious Small Disc

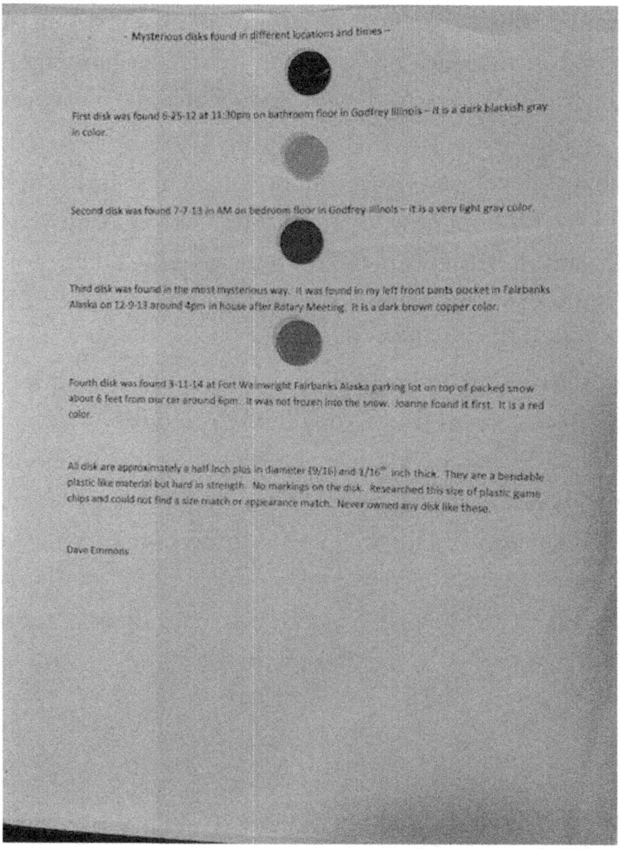

~ Mysterious disks found in different locations and times ~

First disk was found 6-25-12 at 11:30pm on bathroom floor in Godfrey Illinois – it is a dark blackish gray in color.

Second disk was found 7-7-13 in AM on bedroom floor in Godfrey Illinois – it is a very light gray color.

Third disk was found in the most mysterious way. It was found in my left front pants pocket in Fairbanks Alaska on 12-9-13 around 4pm in house after Rotary Meeting. It is a dark brown copper color.

Fourth disk was found 3-11-14 at Fort Wainwright Fairbanks Alaska parking lot on top of packed snow about 6 feet from our car around 6pm. It was not frozen into the snow. Joanne found it first. It is a red color.

All disk are approximately a half inch plus in diameter (9/16) and 1/16" inch thick. They are a bendable plastic like material but hard in strength. No markings on the disk. Researched this size of plastic game chips and could not find a size match or appearance match. Never owned any disk like these.

Dave Emmons

On June 25, 2012, I found this disc on my bathroom floor between my feet while sitting in the bathroom. This was at 11:30 PM before getting ready for bed. I looked down and saw this dark charcoal black disc. I picked it up and measured the disc, and it was nine-sixteenth in diameter and one-sixteenth inch thick. I looked all over my house for something like the disc, but after casually looking for several days, I found nothing like the disc. I kept the disc as a souvenir on my dresser top. It was to be the beginning of more mysteries.

Strange Entities like Jewelry

Seems strange entities like jewelry a lot from my experiences. On July 8, 2013, my silver necklace had a dragonfly trinket hanging on it. The dragonfly trinket disappeared even though the clasp was very tightly attached to the dragonfly. Somebody or something had taken the charm off my necklace while I slept. The chain was sticky to the touch, and I wondered how it got off the necklace. Knowing the past about Apports, I figured an ET or dimensional being borrowed it. The dragonfly is my totem and a good luck charm. Since I have seen several hundred dragonflies flying in groups several times, I felt connected to the dragonfly. They show up when I need a prayer for goals and safety, such as they had when I visited the spiritualist.

My wife and I looked all over the house for the dragonfly charm to no avail. I was still wondering why the chain was so sticky. About a day or so later, the dragonfly charm showed up. Where do these charms go to? This is still a mystery to me about Apports. Where do they go, and how do they get to us? This is a non-stop anomaly that still to this day happens to me. See picture.

Second Disc Shows Up

I took a short nap at 5:10 PM on July 7, 2013, to rest my back. When I woke up at 6:20 PM and got out of bed, I looked down at the bedroom floor while putting my pants on. I was surprised to see another disc lying on the floor in front of me between my feet again. Whoever put it there, placed it where I could easily see it. This disc was the same size and material as the one I found in the bathroom. It feels like a plastic-type material and has the exact measurements as the first one I found—nine sixteenth of an inch in diameter and one-sixteenth inch thick. The color was a light gray color near that of a tan color. I was curious now and wanted to know the answers to these Apports. Finding another disc had a deep meaning to me, and I was excited in a way.

My wife and I looked all over the house for similar objects as these discs but we did not find anything close to them. I researched the internet for game chips like bingo and tiddlywinks but never saw anything the same size or thickness. Most game chips were more extensive and thicker. Games chips were made back in 1888, and they were seven-eighths of an inch in diameter. These thin discs you cannot flip like tiddlywinks. See picture.

Third Disc Put in my Pants Pocket

On December 9, 2013, I went to a Rotary Meeting in Fairbanks, Alaska, with a professor friend of mine. It was a luncheon meeting for the Rotary members and college. It is known that the Fairbanks Alaska College helps the military with their research work. I went to the bathroom, and on the way back, I saw this heavy-set older gentleman in the meeting staring at me. This guy's eyes were piercing, and he stood out, sitting at a table by himself. I felt a strong energy from his stare. I stayed for the two-hour lecture and then my professor friend took me home around 2:30 PM.

I went into my house to change into some warmer clothing and get out of the business casual attire. When I emptied my pants pockets, I pulled out my keys from my left pocket. Something was sticking to my middle finger after pulling out the pocket's contents. It felt sticky, but I discovered it was a third disc, magnetized and sticking to my finger. This disc shook me up. I had chills up and down my spine. I sat on the edge of the bed silent as I looked at another disc. How could it be that these discs are following me from Illinois to Alaska? I called my wife with excitement and told her the weird news of a disc in Alaska. This disc was the exact dimensions as the other two I found, but this one was a copper color and dark brown. I put the three-disc together and considered them priceless. See picture.

Amber Amulet and Necklace Pieces Returned

In January 2014, while I was asleep in Alaska, my Amber Amulet was retaken off the silver chain. The last time a couple of years ago, it disappeared for two days. This particular morning the Amber Amulet was taken off the connecting loop to the chain. But this time, it did not disappear, my wife found it on the floor next to the bed. The clasp was not bent or broken on the chain connector. We both wondered how the Amber Amulet got removed from the chain.

Before the Amber Amulet went missing, I had a short lucid dream. I was with several young humanoids, and as usual, I did not see their faces. One group member approached me with a small rubber-looking hose brown in color. I have seen this hose before during semen collections by ET. I was partially awake, but I knew the magnetic energy sedated me. I am never conscious enough to see or feel how this extraction occurs of my semen—just the reaching for my groin area with a brown hose. I woke up at 5:30 AM the morning of January 21st and felt very worn out and tired. I always remember lucid dreams because they never leave my consciousness.

That same morning, I reached into my change pocket to make sure I had the money for the day. When I pulled out the bills and change, I also had a small Amber jewelry piece stone one-quarter of an inch long and three-sixteenth of an inch wide. A screw accompanied it for jewelry three-eighths of an inch long and three thirty seconds of an inch thick. Both were very small but reminded me of the parts of the necklace I gave to Hiroko in Sedona. More and more, I thought I had an ET visitor with these three occurrences together in the same night. Maybe these were the little calling cards they leave to make you believe you were visited.

Fourth Strange Disc found in Alaska

On March 11, 2014, I found the fourth disc the same size as the other three-disc. This disc was different because it was red. My wife saw this red disc on top of the hard-packed snow in the Base PX Store parking lot. Whoever placed the disc on the ground put it exactly where we would see it. Maybe that is why it was red, so it would show up better on the snow. The red disc was right on my walkway to my car, and they knew we would see it just three feet from my car door.

We were both puzzled about this disc and why are we finding them in Illinois and Alaska. It proved that the ETs can track your location no matter where you are. Frequency tracking of my DNA or an implant giving out radio waves like a GPS. My wife and I had trouble sleeping that night because of the stir over the fourth disc. I was thinking, *why are these discs given to me and what do they want. Are the discs a message I am not understanding?* My electricity was high in my body as usual in bed. I touched my wife, and she said my electricity is hurting her. Having electricity in my body is not unusual, especially after a strange event. See picture.

Chain Found in Pant's Pocket

It seemed the house in Alaska had very high EMF magnetic readings. Alaska is known for magnetic energy, which is one reason why they call it "the Alaskan Triangle". Our living room was 3.5 milligauss' and higher. We often felt uncomfortable in that room. This could be attracting my Apports to our house. On November 26, 2014, I found a short stainless-steel chain about three inches long in my pants pocket. It either came off a small bracelet or a key chain. It could have silver in the metal, I am not sure. I pulled items out of my pants pocket and found this chain. It reminded me of a DNA chain and I have seen chains like this before, but neither one owned a chain like what I found. There is also an Egyptian symbol that means a twine rope or "H" for a hero, like the shape of the small chain. My memory comes back to me from my ledger notes about Hero. Hiroko had mentioned that people call her Hero as a nickname. Could this be a connection? ETs are very much ahead of our understanding. Maybe they communicate with symbols and objects.

Gold Plated Watch Disappeared

On August 13, 2016, back in Illinois after a two-year stay in Alaska, something or somebody, began messing with our jewelry and small articles again. My wife could find a needle in a haystack if she wanted to. If she looks for something and cannot find it, nobody can. My gold-plated watch disappeared. We both looked all over the place in the house and turned up nothing. So, we gave up for a while, and my wife said it would show up somewhere. She was right, but not like she was thinking about it showing up. *Somebody must bring it back,* I thought.

After two weeks of the watch being gone, around the 27th of August, I had a vivid dream that told me where the watch was. The vision told me to look in the top drawer of our dresser by the bed. I thought, *no way. The watch will not be there.* We both had looked at that drawer several times the past two weeks because that is where I typically keep the watch. To my amazement, I looked in the dresser drawer that morning, and there it was, the watch was there in plain sight. It was on top of other items, telling me why we didn't find that watch. It was way too simple where it was located. Do ETs or dimensional beings borrow things and bring them back? This is a borrowed Apport, not a gifted Apport.

Angel Feather Found at Funeral

My fun-loving brother died from cancer way too soon in life—February 5, 2017, at the funeral home where my brother was shown. I was sitting in the front row while people viewed the body of my brother Mick. He had been a good singer and the bass player in our band. Around 3:30 PM, I looked down at the floor and saw a beautiful small white feather between my feet. It was two inches long and one inch wide. I felt this was my brother sending a message from heaven to let me know he was alright where he was. Angel feathers are the same as Apports because they are sent to certain people who are in mourning. Out of nowhere, they will show up. I gave it to my niece sitting beside me and told her, "your dad wants you to have this Angel feather."

More Feathers Found in the House

My wife found two more pure white small feathers the same size, and they are two inches long and one inch wide. On August 21, 2020, she found them in front of her on the steps. We did not have any down or feathered products in the house. It seems feathers and coins are the usual Apport items. If you find anything other than those items, it becomes a more curious experience. I have not listed all the Apports we both have found as they could be considered typical Apports. From what I feel, the Apports I have listed connect with ET and dimensional beings.

20

MYSTERIOUS SCARS AND BRUISES

BRIGHT WHITE LIGHT FLOODING ACROSS MY CAR WINDSHIELD

Early in my travels to the Southwest, I looked for UFOs to capture them on film. On May 27, 2010, on Highway 93 in southern Utah, I turned a curve in the road. As I turned my car, a very bright white light shined into my car's windshield. This light was so bright I could not see anything, and I had to stop my car on the road to avoid crashing. The light seemed to come in the window in waves, and it was hurt my eyes even with sunglasses on. The light hit my right eye the most because I watched the road and stopped the car. Both eyes were burning, so I flushed my eyes with water to make sure I could continue my drive to Alamo, Nevada, for the UFO Convention. My eyes were blurry, but I continued to my destination.

I arrived in Alamo, Nevada, and checked into my room, and the first thing I did was look in the mirror for eye damage. I did not see anything externally, but they were burning. I called my brother Jack to let him know I had reached my destination. My brother was tracking my trip to make sure everything was going alright. This is the same brother who was afraid of me getting abducted due to my past experiences. I told him the time I had, and he asked, "Are you sure about the time?"

"I already adjusted my watch back an hour." I answered.

"You better check your time because you are an hour off in Utah time. You lost an hour, from what I can tell."

"No way!" I hung up with him and called the front desk. The receptionist told me the time was an hour later. I called my brother back and told him he was right about the time. I launched into a story about the bright light flooding my car and mostly burning my right eye. I said it was weird about the light, and I did stop driving but didn't remember anything strange happening.

I went to see an eye doctor at my clinic three weeks later because my right eye still burned. The doctor asked me what had happened to my right eye. I told her a very bright light hit me on a highway in southern Utah. The doctor checked both eyes and kept intensely shining a bright light on my right eye. It was uncomfortable and I told her that the bright light hurts my right eye. The doctor asked me if I did any welding, and to which I responded, "no, I got this burn on the highway in Utah."

"I am just wondering how your retina got so red." She said. She said that was what was burning my eye when she looked at it with light. She spent some time on my right eye, and I was getting a little nervous about what she found. "Your right retina is burned, but it will heal if you use eye drops." She looked curious about how my eye got burned. Knowing doctors don't get into UFOs because of their academic wall, I tried not to say UFO. I jokingly said it might have been a bright light from a UFO ET craft, and I laughed. The doctor just smiled and put in the medical record: *the patient saw a UFO that burned his retina.* I did not see her medical notes until a month later at a follow-up visit for my right eye. There was another doctor this time, and told me it looked like my right eye was much better now. It was then I just happened to see the last doctor's notes, and that is when I saw she mentioned a UFO that burned my eyes. I asked the new doctor why she put UFO in my medical record. He said he wouldn't have put that in the record and I would remove that comment.

If I was abducted in southern Utah, I did not think or feel I was taken. For most of them, I am left with a fact or direct memory regressed for all the abductions. I had no indication this time. Maybe this time was my fifty percent ratio of not knowing anything. I was about thirty miles from Area 51 when the light hit me. On November 15, 2010, there was a regressed dream around 3 AM in bed. This is the only indication I felt something might have happened ET-wise. I woke up holding my right eye and yelling, "Oh no, not my right eye." There was a sharp pain for twenty seconds, and it was over. After that dream, my eye stopped being irritated. This eye had bothered me for six months. The doctor said it would heal slowly. It was hard to absorb what did happen to me in Utah.

Scrapping Scar on my wife's Back

My wife is an academic thinking person and a solid Christian. She knows my experiences and has heard and seen things to validate my high strangeness. You can't be close to an experiencer without knowing some of their events involving the UFO experiences.

On July 21, 2013, my wife said something was touching her in bed while sleeping. I did not experience anything that night, and that is unusual. She woke up with a scrape mark in the lower middle of her back, right on the spine. Looked like a razor scrape about one inch long and one inch wide – almost square. Maybe the ETs were checking her DNA? I don't know. My wife does not want to believe that scenario about ETs, but I can see quite obviously it looks like their work.

She had a previous appointment with a dermatologist, so we asked the doctor about the scrape on her back while she was there. The doctor said she didn't know what the scar was but said it would heal soon, nothing to worry about. It took about six months for the spot to disappear slowly.

Round Red Spots on Arms

After meeting a strange guy at my Lodge in Sedona, Arizona, in 2011, I woke up with round red spots like needle marks. There were two holes on each arm that I did not know where they came from. This

Japanese Guy knew a lot about ETs and even thought the ETs had an attraction for me because of reincarnation. He thought I might be a reincarnated soul they know. He said he liked Sedona for the energy it has in the Buttes. He added that he works with a professor in Tokyo and knows a lot about ETs. I joked with him about dumbing me down, and he looked at me strangely and then told me to have a good night. When I got up the next morning, I had four holes in my arms. Is there a connection?

The reincarnation remark and saying there is no time in the universe made me think this guy is either ET or ET knowledgeable. Maybe he knew Hiroko, my ET friend from Sedona? Perhaps the round marks were his calling card. I never saw him again after that night, even though he was supposed to stay nine days.

Several Round Hole Scars on Left Shin of Left Leg

In Alaska, on August 31, 2014, I had terrible itching on my left leg not far from the ankle. It was sore, so I did not scratch the itchy area. A couple of days later, my wife noticed that there were seven round hole scars on my left shin. They were out of my eyesight, so I did not see them. I looked in the mirror as my wife showed them to me—weird marks, two then two more then three round spots all within the same inch or so area. We took pictures of the scars.

I am familiar with these round hole marks from past events. Usually, three in a row, and that was it. But this time, there were seven holes. I don't do any hard work or hike in the wilderness because of my bad back, so,I know I didn't cause those scars or remember them because it would cause instant pain if I were to hurt myself. See picture.

Strange Marks on Left Leg

While we lived in Alaska, my wife and I both felt the magnetic energy in our house, as I mentioned previously. The nights were also energized because of the tingling and energy flowing up and down my body. I felt rubbing and touching on my arms that made me wake up. I was half asleep and half-conscious when I felt somebody messing with my left leg. I did not feel any pain at that time, but I would see what kind of work the ETs were doing on me the next day —I heard from other ET researchers that the ETs are interested in the left side of the body. Maybe it is a shorter path to the brain and heart. The left side of the brain especially.

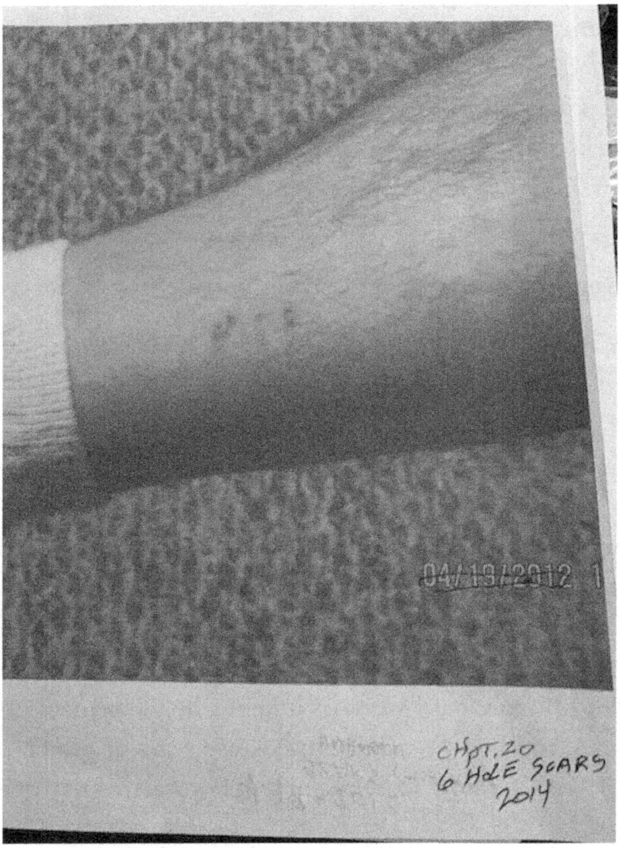

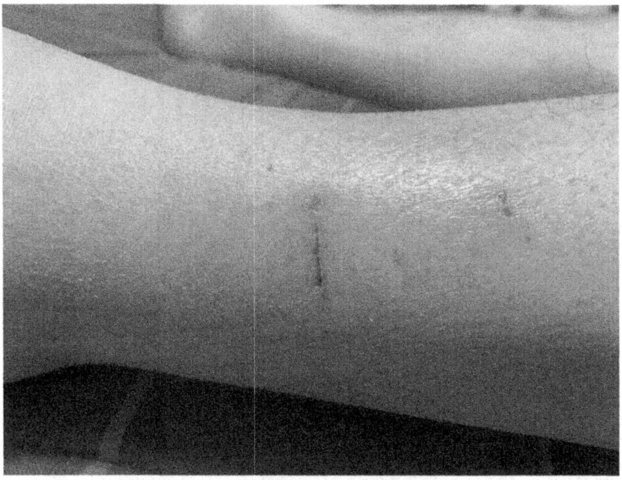

CHAPTER 17
2ND implant
CHPT. 17

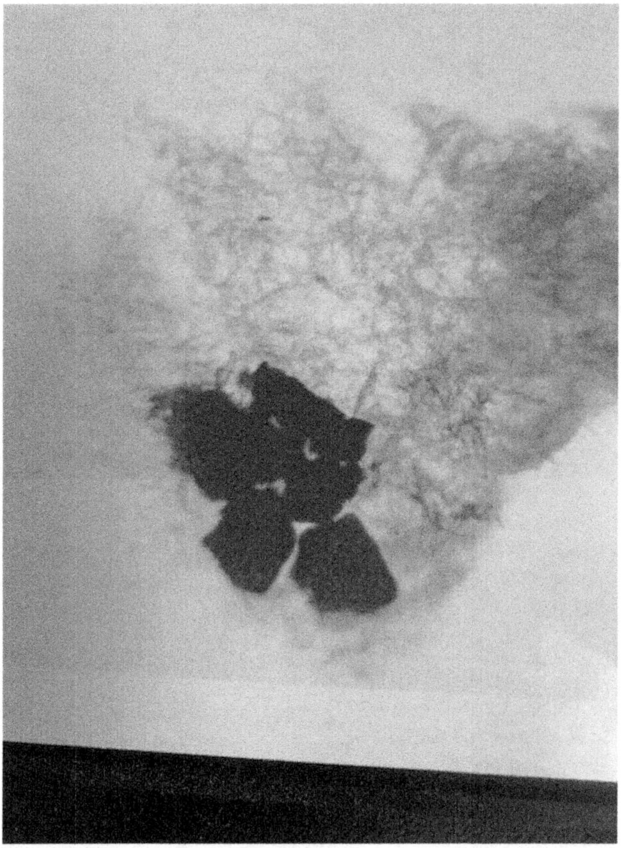

When I got up in the morning, my wife saw six holes in my left lower leg. Small holes but very noticeable and sore to the touch. Again, I did nothing to cause those round marks on my leg because I no longer do hunting or wilderness stuff. The holes were two, two, two, equaling six holes. The bottom two holes were offset from the other four spots. This happened several times in 15 years that I would have marks looking like holes. I got a few scratches on my leg and shoulder and I never figured out how I got them. I took pictures of all these marks, but I will write them in the book instead of putting pictures so as to allow more room in my book.

Wife's Left Shoulder Marks Handprints

My wife seldom talks about the strangeness that I have been involved in over the years she has been with me. She would wake me up and ask me if I touched her or rubbed on her.

"No, it was not me, honey," was always my response. I never play around while she is sleeping, especially to scare her. She had the typical red marks that I get in bed a lot. Like finger pokes or tips of finger pressure. There were two thumbs like red spots and four minor red needle-looking marks.

This time, her arm's left triceps and shoulder areas had red round marks and smaller red holes. The smaller holes looked like needle marks or sensitive test equipment. This took place in Alaska in 2014, where we felt the energy. She looked nervous about her arm marks. She asked me if they would hurt us.

"Who are 'they'?" I asked her, a little confused.

"It is your ET buddies." She responded.

"I have not been hurt badly by them in years. They won't hurt us, honey." I tried to ease her anxieties. I wish I could have been more upfront with her about ETs, but she does not like talking about that subject. She always tells me to believe in God, and they will go away. I imparted that I don't think it is that easy. This was not her first experience of something near her that was strange. I don't like my ET friends to mess with my wife, but nothing stops them.

Bruises and Small Red Marks on My Right Shoulder

On July 25, 2015, I had a very stirring night in Alaska. I felt like I was rolled around in bed in all positions. This was undoubtedly an abduction event after seeing the bruises the next day. My right shoulder was bruised near the shoulder blade, and another bruise continued down my arm six inches. There were tiny red needle marks like I described before intertwined with the bruises. My arm and shoulder felt sore like I had arm-wrestled. But hell, maybe I did wrestle with something.

I remember a tingling sensation before the movement of my body. I was very familiar with this energy going through my body by this time and knew I was being dumbed down or anesthetized. I also knew I went unconscious in bed after this energy hit me. It is difficult to know how long you have been unconscious in bed. You might look at the clock when you were awakened, but you won't know the exact moment when you went unconscious. Usually, you are exhausted and still sleepy and you won't notice the marks on your body for a couple of hours unless you have blood on your sheets. Drops of blood were usually noticed right away when I put the bedsheets back together in other events. This night with bruises, I did not see blood.

Scratches on My Left Shoulder

Between 2016 and 2019, I had numerous accounts of sounds and touches on my body: body freezing and lucid dreams. I won't get into all the dreams; I will save that for another time. I also have pictures of these scars but too numerous to list images. This period in 2020 was a busy time with ET visitors. I heard my motion sensors go off downstairs. Listened to a clicking sound in my ear and outside of my ear. My wife heard these same sounds and asked me what they were. "Maybe my friends are back." I responded. After that, we fell back to sleep again. The reptilians make a chattering metallic sound and a clicking sound around you. I will discuss this in more depth towards the end of my 2020 and 2021 experiences.

My trail camera (with infrared ability) was taking pictures of the many orbs that set the cameras off, which I found that out the following day. Later I will discuss why I had the cameras at the ready. I have spoken to a lot of Abductees in interviews on the radio. There are commonalities with all of us. A clicking sound is heard in the ear and outside of the ear. I started having a lucid dream that I was trained to enter a pipe or transfer tube to travel somewhere else. It was 5 AM when I awoke.

After I woke up, I noticed my left shoulder being sore when I moved it around. I looked at the shoulder and saw three red scratch marks that I knew I did not cause. The scratches were two inches to three inches long. The scratches look like three fingers with sharp claws or fingernails. That is when I knew something had happened this night involving ETs. When I checked my trail cams, I found some film blanked out but found videos of orbs floating all over the room. There was a bunch of activity that night.

More Scratches, Bruises, and Small Holes in Skin

July 29, 2021, I was in bed sleeping around midnight. I felt a bad stinging sensation that woke me up. It was an itchy feeling on my left leg three inches above the ankle inside of calve area. This area hurt for two days, and swelled up like a mosquito bite, but there were no mosquitoes. What woke me up was the stinging pain and nerve endings firing off my leg. I felt weak and like my blood was rushing throughout my body. My wife took pictures of the two puncture-types small holes in the skin with swelling around them. The tiny puncture holes in the skin were beginning to be a recurring event presently and in the past. What are these round puncture wounds that can't be explained while sleeping? Likely blood drawing by ETs or implants that modify our DNA.

Starting October 10, 2021, I call them the very active four months of 2021. I had various strange dreams and ET in nature with noises like clapping, door knocks, and clicking in the ear. I woke up from the dreams causing me to stir in fear. I went downstairs and noticed my left forearm had a bruise on it with three small red holes lined up perfectly. These round small red holes were not new to me, so I figured it meant ET was messing with me again. In 2020 and 2021, I still experienced ET activity even after all these years. My arm looked like it was twisted by someone or something while sticking me with whatever, I don't know. My question was, why me and why the marks on the body? It takes about a week for these scars to go away.

On October 12, 2021, I found even more scars on my left leg during another busy night. I felt restless trying to sleep because I felt a presence near me in the bed. I was wondering, *alright, what is next*? I fell into a sound sleep and did not know what had happened that night. Until, as I said, I found a long scratch on my left leg when I woke up. Here we go again, left leg and left side. This was good enough evidence to tell me ETs were in my bedroom again. My wife did not notice anything that night. The scratch was two inches long but had four holes linked with the scratch. These unusual holes were embedded in the scratch because scratches and red holes are mostly separate marks. There were two holes above the scratch. For a day, my leg was sore, and I documented the marks and scars through photos.

From laser thin cut lines on the body for implants to small red holes, scraping off the skin, and long scratches with spots in the scratch itself. These are the scars that I have no idea where they came from. If I don't do much hiking or rough work, so how do I get these marks while sleeping in a bed. And how does my wife get scars while sleeping that she cannot figure out. My conclusion is that these scars were made by ETs or dimensional beings for testing of our bodies or DNA manipulating. Most scars coincide with abduction activity or touching from beings that have interceded with humans for thousands of years. Only God of these gods knows the truth about all life in the universes.

21

STRANGE PEOPLE WALKING AMONGST US

STRANGE MEN AT AN ARKANSAS UFO CONVENTION

On April 8, 2010, I attended an annual UFO Convention in Arkansas. My friends and I would travel together and have a good time for three days at the convention. We knew many of the regular attendees, but sometimes you see strange people that look out of place. There were these two men that nobody saw coming or going in the parking lot. They were there only one day of the convention. One was a short older man in his early fifties with an old wool sportscoat and old baggy trousers. It looked like he just jumped in this present time from the 1950s. His face was wrinkled and pale-looking, and he had gray, blonde hair. He also wore an outdated hat. If I had to guess, he looked to be a professor type. His partner was a tall younger man, standing at about six feet three inches tall. This guy wore a black sportscoat with black pants and looked the part of a large bodyguard. He had dark hair and a Caucasian complexion, and looked average compared to his partner.

These two sat directly in front of my friends and me. The younger bodyguard guy was laughing to himself without anyone talking to him. I think he knew I was watching him from behind. I thought they might be Convention speakers. So, I asked the two, "are you two speakers"? The older guy turned and gave me a dirty look and said,

"NO" very forcefully. I noticed the younger man wore thick sunglasses with some attachment in the middle of the glasses. They seemed interested in the late Jim Marrs and what he had to talk about. Strangely, these two did not speak to anybody at the convention. My friends asked me to take pictures of them and find out who they were.

I followed them out to where Jim Marrs was selling his latest book during the break. These two strange guys stood near Jim's table, looking at him without talking. They would stare at each other like telepathically communicating. The younger man had a small black device in his right hand about five inches long and one inch or so in diameter. I wondered what that device was and its purpose. Maybe it was a dumbing down tool like I saw in a regressed dream twice. However, it could have been a mind-reading tool that they used on Jim Marrs. When I took pictures of these two strange men, I acted like I was taking pictures of my friends in line with the two unknown guys. When I took my first picture of them, the older man looked at the big young guy and told him I was taking pictures of them. I wondered how he knew I was taking pictures without looking in my direction. The larger young guy turned and gave me a mean angry look as I took a picture of him looking at me. I was able to take two photos of these two strange guys.

Usually, I will wait for a couple of facts to turn up before making an opinion of what I see. The older man went to the bathroom soon after that, so I followed him to check him out up close. When I walked into the bathroom just a few seconds after him, he was not in the bathroom – he had disappeared. I stood there washing my hands, waiting for him to show up but he was gone. My friends asked me what I found out and if I got photos of them. I said I got a couple of pictures earlier, but I was puzzled by how the older man had just disappeared in the bathroom. I told them people did not see them come and go to the convention hall. Well, I found out how they travel. I told them they disappear and go back to their craft. They were men in black, I told them. LMH told me they always have one or two strange people at each convention.

Brother Jack and I at St. Louis Museum

My brother Jack and I went to the St. Louis Art Museum on August 19, 2010, to see the Egyptian display. We were slowly going around each presentation and looking at the artifacts, taking our time. We both loved Egyptian art and Egyptian building skills. As we looked at the displays, I felt we were being watched. I turned around and saw a middle-aged man in his fifties who was slightly overweight watching us. He had on a white shirt and wore khaki pants. He was about five feet eleven inches tall with dark, piercing eyes. His face was a typical man of his age but had a strange stare. He had no museum badge on or ID hanging on a lanyard so, he did not work for the museum. He had his hands behind his back most of the time. He must have watched us for three minutes total. I must have turned and looked at him three times and caught him staring at us. I asked my brother to look around at this guy without noticing that we knew he was watching us. My brother said, "yes, he is weird. He was watching us."

When the "Watcher" noticed us noticing him, he quickly started walking around another display case. I noticed he had a slight limp in the right leg.

"Let's follow him to see where he goes." I told my brother. Both of us quickly followed him around the back display case. When we got to where he was walking, he was gone. He disappeared as he walked around the corner.

"That is impossible. Where did he go?" My brother was incredulous.

"He was not one of us. He was a "Watcher," and he was interested in us for some reason." I said to my brother, "I had seen these strangers disappear before my eyes several times." *Are they dimensional beings?* we asked each other.

I said "Watcher" because of the Fallen Angel story in the Bible where Angels would watch us, humans. There is a story in the Bible that Watchers took care of Jesus. When he was at a dinner with his followers, two watchers warned him of Romans approaching. Are they still here but a great deal more of them to watch over us?

Stranger at Bass Pro Shop

I was shopping for travel clothes for my upcoming trip to the southwestern US. It was March 30, 2011, and I was looking at cargo shorts at Bass Pro men's clothing area. While I was at the turnstyle shorts rack, a man about mid-forties of age and about six feet three inches tall stood nearby. He wore an expensive suit and had close-cropped hair, almost a burr haircut. He was white and pale-looking but normal complexion. He wore an expensive suit and tie. He seemed to be an agent as in FBI or NSA agent. He stood on the other side of the shorts rack and kept staring at me. He was not shopping at all and if I had to judge by his looks, he does not shop at Bass Pro.

This strange man must have stood there staring at me for two minutes. I felt like I wanted to say something to him, but my tongue would not move. I felt dumbed down and not myself, or I would have said something to him. He finally walked away quickly, and I followed him as fast as possible. The strange man walked around the next aisle, and he was gone. He disappeared almost right in front of me. Was he a MIB or a dimensional "Watcher"? It would have to be a new version of MIB because he was not dressed in black because it was a gray suit he had on. Was he a walk-in ET or shapeshifting reptilian? People that look like normal human beings but have powers that we don't understand like disappearing.

Alaska Time Travelers in Large Store

In March of 2014, my wife and I went to the large department store in Fairbanks, Alaska. This location seemed to be the meeting place for Fairbanks's residents to talk and see each other. Since it is so cold in Fairbanks, often this was a warm place for them to talk. I sat at the doorway, waiting for my wife to pick up some jewelry from a shop around the corner from where I was seated. This store was huge and had everything you needed, so many people enjoyed shopping there. I saw many different people from other countries shopping in the store and some just meandering in the large store. I have seen strange things happen in Fairbanks, but what I saw that day still bothers me.

To give some backstory info, it would seem my third eye and the pineal gland were activated to see and to hear strange dimensional events. My wife said I could see what others couldn't because of my third eye. If people would be more observant and conscious of their surroundings, they too can see strange people and events. My combat experience in the U.S. Army taught me to be hyper-alert of my surroundings. This is what the word consciousness means and why it is essential for ET communications.

I saw two people, both around forty years old standing close together and well dressed. The lady had a long dress and nice high heels on. The guy had a very nice suit on that would cost some money at the clothing store. They stuck out from the rest of the customers who were dressed warmly with several layers of clothing. I thought, *alright, they were here to speak at the College of Fairbanks.*

What caught my attention that was so unusual? First, they stood so close to each other, facing one another like they were going to kiss. Secondly, the guy had something in his right hand that was put in between the two of them. This object's top was spinning, and they were both looking at it. They were attempting to hide this object with their bodies, hoping people would not see them with a spinning object, though I could. I could also see they talked very low to each other where nobody could hear them. When I first noticed the strange couple, it seemed they just appeared out of nowhere. Strangely standing in the middle of the front entrance, it seemed as though they were by themselves. People were walking around them, not paying attention, not looking at them.

My mind seemed not to respond to this strange scene, it felt like I was supposed to be quiet. This couple stood close for several minutes with the spinning device between them. Then the man put something in his coat pocket on the right side of his body. I was positioned looking at their left sides, unable seeing what he put away. They got two coffee cups from the deli and strolled into the store. I did not see them again after they walked away. My thoughts were that there are a lot of military research projects in and around the Army base and the College of Alaska. Maybe this couple was time travelers, and the spinning device was a time GPS? When you see people out of place and seem like they don't belong, they could be time travelers or ET Watchers.

These stories are accurate and true, but I can't be decisive about who they are. Their purpose eludes me also. I see these strange people walking amongst us very infrequently – not a lot.

A Woman I met in Sedona Admitted She Was a Hybrid ET

On June 24, 2011, I met an extraordinary person in Sedona, Arizona. While waiting in line for my pizza I ordered for myself, the lodge manager, a tall black woman, walks in behind me. She got in behind me in line to wait for her order. The woman, who I will refer to as "C", said hello to me, very friendly. Strangely enough, she told me she knew I would be here in this pizza shop. She followed up by saying she was told to meet me here, and we're supposed to meet. *Yes,* I said to myself, *I have heard that said before from another humanoid ET,* Hiroko. This lady looked forty years old but had a younger aura about her. "C" was about five foot and eleven inches tall with short dark hair. She had large eyes and was an attractive woman. She seemed like a lovely person. I asked her why she said we are supposed to meet. This is when she flat out told me she was an alien hybrid person whose purpose was to communicate with humans and enlighten humans. "C," said her guides told her to meet me, and she was led to me by my energy.

I asked her questions, of course, about being an alien hybrid. She said she has babies and gives them to the ETs as hybrid children. "C," said she gives the babies up after three months, the first trimester to the ETs. She told me she was a psychiatric nurse for a psychiatrist husband for which she divorced. She showed me pictures of her three kids and ex-husband that she carried with her. I had a hard time believing those were her real family. I asked her if she lived in Sedona. She said yes, she is living with her sister in town. I somewhat did not believe that statement either. She told me our meeting was synchronicity.

I also asked her where she travels to. She answered Florida, Hawaii, Australia, Mexico, and the Bahamas all over the earth. She was very convincingly. I asked her how she affords traveling like what she does. She said the places she goes to, others like her, take care of her. "Others" meaning ET hybrids she meets up with in all these locations. She asked me if I wanted to meet later for a drink. I declined, "No thanks. I am leaving early in the morning." She gave me her full name and phone contact. "C," told me to look her up on FaceBook. Before she left, she told me I was full of energy from the ETs contacting me. She knew too much about ETs and hybrids and people like her across the globe. It made me more curious about her real life.

We followed each other on Facebook and, yes, she had pictures of all these places she mentioned to me in her travels. Until I got married several years ago, I followed her travels on FaceBook. She was a teacher of energy meditation and explained some of the ET contacts I had over the years. She said that ETs put implants in people to store memories of their kind in our bodies. She also mentioned reincarnation that the ETs use in our matrix within a matrix, meaning two souls can join one biological body for storage. Maybe that is why scientists can't explain all our wasted DNA? "C" was an extraordinary person.

Strange Hooded Humanoid Dressed in Black Encounter

I met with a friend involved in spiritualism at a restaurant in St. Louis near the Barnes Hospital area. Her name is also "C." We established a good friendship and became research partners in ETs and spirituality. We just had a light dinner and talked about spirituality and meditation. She had spiritual training and knew about other dimensions. Her occupation was an engineer, and she was very talented in what she did in her career. We left the restaurant at 9:30 PM with her going down the sidewalk to her car. My car was parked in front of the restaurant, so, I did not have far to walk to my car. Out of concern for her safety, I watched her walk to her car.

I pulled my car up to the exit area of the parking lot. As soon as I pulled up to the edge of the road, a tall man dressed in all black with a black hood over his head walked in front of my car. He turned and looked at me, his face a dark greenish color with big eyes staring at me. He was about six foot five inches tall and very thin-looking. The most striking thing I saw was his face. I have to say he was horrid and evil-looking, like a shapeshifting reptilian. He stopped in front of my car and stared at me. I froze and thought, *what is this thing*? It was like he was sending me a message – a message telling me to be careful what I find out in my ET studies. His eyes said, "*stop what you are doing*" as he knew what our conversations were about inside the restaurant. The whites of his eyes were big and bold, but his face appeared olive green in color. I thought he might approach me, but I think he saw others in the lot, which made him back off. I was terrified of this thing or humanoid ET.

He remained stopped in front of the car. He paused and stared at me four more times before leaving the area. Each time he looked at me, it seemed he was sending a message to me to stop my ET research. This caused a fearful gut feeling because I felt his negative energy pulsing at my car. He had a negative aura about him and was out of place in this part of town – west St. Louis. It is scary when you feel evil staring down at you. I slowly pulled out of the parking lot, watching if he would show up again to menace my fears more.

I talked to my friend "C" later that night by cell phone and asked her if she saw this strange guy. She said yes, he passed her on the sidewalk, walking very fast like he was walking with a purpose. She said he looked ugly and scared her. "C" is an empath and can read negative energy around people. She thought he was extraordinary. I told her I was glad he did not attack either one of us. I was ready if he did, but I could not imagine what kind of powers he held being a shapeshifter. We both knew of his negative energies just by being close to him. I wondered if he could have been a MIB, but he did not dress like men in black do.

Another Strange Encounter at a UFO Meeting

I frequented a UFO meeting in St. Louis County that my friend "R" held once a month. On June 4, 2012, around 6:10 pm, the typical people and typical meeting agenda discussed UFOs and ETs. We shared stories and experiences of UFOs; this meeting had a different kind of attendee that people noticed right away. My friend "R" told me this strange man showed up early but never spoke introduced himself. The strange man sat by himself, and nobody sat next to him. He even looked different from all the rest of us.

This strange man observed everybody like a robot would look at a human. He was about five feet eight inches tall, with a slimly built body. He had short red hair and looked fifty years old by earth years. The man's face looked pale and had rough-like skin. His eyes were dark and piercing. I won't forget his stare as he sat about ten feet away from my table with friends. While I went to pick up a food order, he asked my lady friend "G," who was sitting with me at my table, if I was her husband. She told him no, I was just a friend. When I came back to my table, my friend "G" told me what he had asked her. I said, "wow, he spoke." She said that is all he said.

Some of the ladies at the meeting asked how could a hybrid ET mess up red hair dye. His hair had a strange red color and seemed like a wig of some kind. His stare was powerful and stopped most of us from questioning him. His energy was repelling us but at the same time he was observing us intently. Another Buddy "R" also believed he was a hybrid or non-human of some kind. These people in the meeting knew about ET studies. Nobody talked to him, and nobody was inclined to. So, twenty-five people had the same impression about this man that he was not human. This strange man listened intently to our discussions but never spoke out. He left the meeting early, causing our group to make him our ET topic for another half hour. These strange people have the same operational approach to humans. They are quiet and say few words but observe us, humans, closely. They tend to make humans peaceful with their energies like a partial dumb-down effect. They walk amongst us humans to learn how to be more like us. If you are alert and conscious of these strangers, you will see them.

22

LUCID REGRESSED DREAMS

TWO HOODED PRIEST

Starting with the year 2010, it seemed I began having more often than normal, lucid, ET-related dreams. In December 2010, I had an obvious lucid dream that came with a message. I dreamed of two hooded and robed Priest or Religious leaders telepathically communicating to me. They appeared to be the old priest that wore long robes with a hood over their head. I found myself on the floor of a small block building with a sand floor. In my mind, I felt like it was around the time of Jesus' 30 AD. It was a small meeting building for church prayer meetings.

I pulled bronze fishing hooks out of the sand and put them in a grass sack. I had two kids playing around me and clinging to my shoulders. There was a tall, hooded man in the corner of the building and the size of the building was about thirty feet by thirty feet square. The hooded priest in the corner started walking out on a block ledge surrounding the floor about four feet wide on all four sides of the building. As he was walking out, another priest dressed in a robe and hood walked past him to take his place at the corner where he stood. As the priest stood in the corner of the building, he told me telepathically that he was my new pastor. This priest went on to say, *clean the church up, take care of the children, and you don't have to attend church* telepathically.

While I watched these priests exchange positions, I dug brass fishing hooks out of the sand floor. These hooks were more significant than our modern hooks. Later, I looked them up on the internet and found them precisely what I was picking up. The bronze hooks were roughly cast with some jagged edges on them. The hooks were about two and a half inches long and three-eighths inch wide. The kids were still playing around me and giggling, having fun in the sand. I asked the new priest, now standing in the corner of the building, "where were Jack and P?"

"They went fishing together." He answered. Jack is my brother, and "P" was an old friend. Why I brought his name up is beyond me?

I always truth check lucid dreams. I expect a fact to come out of the dream in order for it to be legitimate. I went to the gym and met an old friend, and I told him about my dream.

"R," how is "P" doing because he was mentioned in my vision by a priest or maybe even Jesus the other night." I asked.

"You have not heard about "P"?" "R" asked, "he has cancer in three places on his body. He is not doing good."

"Wow, I need to call him and tell him that I dreamed of Jesus and mentioned his name."

I called "P" that day, and he said he wasn't doing so good, and his cancer was spreading. I asked "P" if he believes in God. He said yes, he did and I told him my whole dream.

"It is unusual that you called me today because I skipped my chemo medicine today at the hospital," "P," said.

"If you believe in God, keep taking the chemo meds and fight this cancer," I implored him.

"This call is weird. I will start my chemo back tomorrow and fight this cancer." "P" said, "Thank you so much."

My facts seemed to be correct on this lucid dream because I was told about "P" in the dream. I also was right about the building structure and the bronze hooks. The ET I met the month before putting my lucid dream into my subconscious. ETs leave tidbits of information for me to absorb. My friend did succumb to cancer some months later, but I was glad I got to talk to him about God.

Regressed Dream of being a Grandfather to Hybrid Kids

During that same month of May in 2011, I found myself in a large room with kids playing in the room. I was asleep when this dream happened. A deep sleep will put me in a regressed dream mode most of the time. Hypnosis does not work for me, so I bring regression from actual incidents into my subconscious. This particular instance, a young humanoid boy was playing around with me as kids do. There were other children hybrid types in this large room. I was telepathically told to be a Grandfather to them and train them in human emotions. I have never seen or remembered their faces, only that they wore the usual white smock thick material like a gown.

This young boy hurt my leg somehow, and I pushed him away, telling him that was not nice. His reaction was to use a tractor beam toy on a small scale. I felt this buzzing and snapping sound at my back. It did not hurt or burn my back, but it raised me in the air. I felt weightless, and that was a great feeling. His toy was about five inches long and black like a small flashlight. Then the boy turned it off, and I hit the floor hard, but I was not hurt. Not bad to not getting hurt because I was up about six feet off the floor. He seemed to be six or seven years old, and this levitation toy was meant to train him to use larger devices.

The boy walked away after that, so I guess the playing was over. Being in big rooms training kids was not my first regressed dream of this kind. I wish I could see their faces, but I guess they don't want me to. My thoughts were, so, this is where human parents meet hybrid kids once in their lifetimes. Dreams are difficult to figure out. Do we travel with our soul and consciousness to other places at night? A scientific friend tells me that this dream meant I am missing something. Regressed dreams are typically so realistic you think you are at that very place. I knew, fully, that I had been abducted numerous times but could not relate the regressed dream to the abduction. There is often a delay with dreams in time, and it is not easy to pinpoint the abduction event associated with the dream.

Regressed Dream of being on a Supply UFO Ship

This regressed dream specifically happened in October 2012. I was tossing about in bed and murmuring words that made no sense, my wife said. This was at the end of the recalled event of being on an ET ship. I ended up standing on top of a stairway overlooking the transporting device and suppl area. The large room was dimly lit and there were two small entities about four feet six inches tall looking up at me. They had white space suits on with yellow helmets. I could see their faces, and while they looked like young kids, I knew they were adult ET by their actions. They had blue eyes. I felt no fear from seeing these ETs. They were very docile and calm.

In my ledger, I called them babyfaces because they reminded me of young kids. They had a light pale complexion with small noses and mouths. Simply very human-looking ETs with peace in their telepathic communications with me and I was made to feel at ease.

Since they were in helmets, I could not see their complet appearance. I looked around and saw what looked to be large boxes and other objects stored on their ship. There was some movement around the ship, but I did not see them up close due to the distance – such a large ship.

I watched these two small ETs walk towards a glassed-in semicircular room about four feet off the floor. They joined two other ETs with yellow helmets and white spacesuits. They carried a case-looking object with hoses and wires going into their suits. This was clearly a transporter room as you could see the ETs standing, then they disappeared very fast. They were no doubt being transported to another location or planet via teleportation.

My regressed dream ended when they were transported. For some reason, I was supposed to see this. When I got put back in my bed, there was magnetic energy in the bed that I measured three milligauss on my tri-field meter. I had the meter sitting by my bed because of all the magnetic energy in the house, and when these events happened, there was an increase in magnetic energy. As we know, the ways they are used to transport us are magnetic energy and electricity.

23

FAMILY ET CONNECTIONS AND WITNESSES

MOTHER'S ET EXPERIENCES

My mother, ninety-four years old with excellent mental acuity, started telling me her ET experiences when she was eighty years old. She told me she had tall, slender, and black shadowy figures coming up her hallway to her bedroom. Suddenly, she fell off into a deep sleep after she felt something touch her body. My mother even said they were molesting her in her younger years. The molestation even happened in her eighties and up to the last few years. Being her son, she would not go into detail about these instances. My brothers asked me why she only tells me about these experiences, and I replied that she knows I understand because I am an experiencer. My mother said tall, dark slender figures had visited her throughout her life and she never saw their faces. That sounds familiar and accurate to my past experiences.

While visiting my mother on May 4, 2012, she told me more experiences about another type of strange entity that visited her. These shadowy figures were tall, bald, deep-set dark eyes, and pale, a little different type of ET this time. Maybe tall white ETs were visiting her on these occasions. My mother was eighty-five years old at this time but still had a great memory. She said they would mostly come into her bedroom while my dad worked midnights. Even after my dad passed in 1995, the visitations still occurred. She told me you would not believe what she saw in her house. This is a strong old-school woman that nothing scares her in everyday life. She gave birth to eleven children and knew how to handle herself emotionally.

On May 28, 2012, I told my mother about my lucid dreams about ETs. I told her I felt something heavy sit by me in bed. My mother said, "Oh my, the same thing happened to me around the same time." She told me something sat by her early that morning, and she felt the bed sink way down under the weight of it. She heard a clicking sound in her ears before she felt the bed sink down. She was unable to tell if the clicking came from outside her body or her ears. I explained I have the same clicking sounds and don't know if they are outside my body or ears. So, we both have the same sounds and experiences with our strange visits. I told her we have a lot in common on sounds before they touch us. Other abductees say they also hear clicking sounds during their events. My mother does not keep up with others' experiences, so how did she know? After the clicking, she said she felt like she was being grabbed and touched by these ET visitors. Like my visitors, she did not see their faces. It was strange we both had similar experiences.

My mother and other family members experienced a UFO sighting together on July 9, 2015, in the early evening. My mother called to tell me that sister Sherry and brother Jay saw a long cylinder object floating over the neighborhood close to where I lived. At the time, I was in Alaska. My mother said it was flying slow just at the tops of the trees on the street. She told me this tubular/cylinder-shaped UFO was as long as eight houses on the road and it was a dark gray color. She said it moved just a little, stayed there for a few seconds, and then quickly vanished. My mother said my brothers and sister had seen these crafts occasionally around their area. Brother Jay said he saw an antenna on this massive craft at the top.

On September 22, 2020, my mother, sister Sherry and brother Terry saw a bright metallic shining craft fly over their neighborhood. My mother said this UFO was not as large as they had seen in the past and that this craft flew over their house a week before. So, in essence, they saw the same UFO twice, flying over their house. It flew from east to west both times. The craft was so bright they could not make out a definitive shape except that it looked round and was very bright in the sun. My other brother Jan has seen several crafts in the same area, and by proxy, you could say this might be a portal area. He had seen a box-type UFO, giant triangle UFO, and a circular object within months of each sighting. This was a road close to my mother's house. Maybe these sightings by all my family might prove at least to my family that ETs follow family DNA frequencies. My family has seen enough strange craft to be good eyewitnesses.

My mother told me that her family had seen UFOs, the flying saucer type, as far back as the late forties and fifties. One was in their backyard at my grandmother's house. They all got scared and did not want to move around in the house. She never said the ETs entered the house, it just hovered in their yard. Family DNA frequencies and Native American Indians tend to also be targets of ETs research projects from recent research on abductions. My mother is one-third Crowe Indian, making us siblings about twelve percent Indian. Could that be a possibility?

My mother told me a year ago of the latest strange events in her house. She said she saw a five-foot-tall, bright gold Buddha-looking figure in her hallway. My mother said she heard a noise that woke her up and saw this brilliant shiny figure in her hall. She felt spiritual in how she perceived this object. This happened in 2020, so even still she has strange events occuring. She said she still feels somebody grabbing her feet at night and touching her. The same thing happens to me at night as mentioned. They pull on your feet to wake you up from sleep. This could occur after doing some DNA or blood work at your bedside.

In 2021, my mother saw a man with denim pants and a white t-shirt like someone from the fifties. She saw him walk right past her as if she wasn't even there. She said he was white in skin color with dark hair. She also still feels someone heavy sitting next to her to this date. Could this be a past relative, dimensional entity, or an ET masked as a human? My mother is very intuitive, and you cannot hide anything from her when she looks at you—a gift or a menace, it all depends on how you look at it. If you have had experiences with ETs, you are left with enlightenment as it opens your third eye.

My mother and my sister Sherry and Royce (brother-in-law) saw a tall MIB in the field behind my house. We had several family members living on the same street. They saw him at different angles and described precisely what he looked like. My brother-in-law is a skeptic, and he told me he finally saw something weird. He was with my sister getting ready to leave their house when it happened. My mother said he was very tall and wore a long black coat with a black hat. The wind was blowing hard, and he was standing at the beginning of a storm in this field. They all said he was bent down, digging something up from the ground that was freshly cultivated. My mother, sister, and brother-in-law watched him for a minute or so, as they say. They thought it was strange being close to my backyard in the field.

My mother also said she saw a dark figure sitting in my chair on my front porch. That it seemed to be waiting for me to come home. My sister saw the exact dark figure behind my car one evening while I was gone in my truck. They both feared me being around those dark entities around my house. It is not the first time people have seen dark figures following me or waiting for me, one of spirtualists had mentioned it as well. I don't feel these dark objects are evil. I have no feeling of evilness around me. So, maybe ETs are in an invisible cloaked mode?

Other Witnesses that Saw Strange Objects Around My House

A Solid Object Brushing Against Feet

My friend I will call D1, told me about his experience staying in my spare bedroom one night. We both just finished at a UFO Convention in Arkansas when he told me about the incident that occurred in April 2010. He wanted to target practice with my John

Wayne Winchester rifle the next day. I thought everything went well with breakfast and the range. On February 17, 2011, he told me on the phone about his experience in my spare bedroom the year before. He said he was holding back the information because he didn't want to scare me or bother me with this event. I reassured him that I had scary moments before, and it would not bother me. He told me that he could not sleep the night he spent at my house. There was something in his room that he felt was strange. He felt something solid and heavy brush up against his feet in bed. He said this happened several times during the night, so leading him to not sleep well. D1 used to be a ghost hunter, so he knew this was no ghost. He repeated that "this was no ghost" very strongly, it was solid and human-like in its walking motion. I was nonplussed and told him it is probably an ET that watches over me and observes me. I again reassured him that I was fine, there was no bother telling me this information. That I knew what it was that messed his night up. They brush up against me too and grab my leg or feet occasionally. They are ETs.

Orange – Yellow Light in Field

The following story comes from a neighbor, "J" as I will call him, in Godfrey, Illinois. On October 10, 2011, he told me that he and his girlfriend saw a yellowish-orange light in the field in the back of my house. He said the light was swaying back and forth like a lantern with someone walking with it, but he did not see anybody holding the lantern. "J," said the light did not shine on the trees or ground. The orange light was at a distance in the field behind my house and his house. "J," told him, and his girlfriend watched this yellow, orange light for an hour until 1 AM.

Sounds and Light in Backyard

My neighbors on the other side of my house, I will call them "A" and "S" in Godfrey, Illinois. They both told me a week after the event in my front yard about their experience. On October 22, 2011, they finally told me about the event. I had experiences around this time with abductions, so it fits the timeline. They said they heard a humming sound a week ago at around 1:30 AM. They agreed this humming sound lasted thirty minutes. "A," said he checked all over his house for intruders and found nothing. They felt that someone was doing something in their backyard, which our properties are next to each other. Both said their bedroom window was vibrating and making noise. And yet, they could not figure out the humming source. Neither one wanted to look outside to see what was going on. They were both terrified and did not have the nerve to look outside. Both said there were lights flickering along with the humming sound. They asked me if I was alright because they knew of my experiences, and now because of this they were believers. I told them I did not hear or see anything around 1 AM. No doubt I was the target that night for an ET visit, but both said they could not sleep because of the incident scaring them.

Bright Cone Shaped Light in my Backyard

Once again, my neighbor "J" came over to my front porch to tell me something. This was on September 7, 2012, and he said he was afraid to tell me about this event. He did not want to alarm me or scare me about what happened a month ago. "J," said he saw a bright white light about fifteen feet in diameter in my backyard around 2:30 AM. The light lasted only ten seconds. He said it seemed to start smaller higher up like a cone; then the light spread out about fifteen feet on the ground. "J" was at his bathroom window when he saw this in my backyard facing the light. He asked me if I saw anything, and I said no. He went on saying, "This was weird, man." He expressed hope that he did not scare me, and I responded, "No! Thanks a lot, neighbor."

My Thoughts About What the Witnesses Told me

At the same time my neighbors told me about their strange events around the back of our houses, I personally was experiencing abductions and a lot of activity in and out of my house. In my front yard, I saw different color orbs varying in size, and the colors were primarily white, but there were blue and red orbs. These orbs appeared in my house, in my hallway and seemed to follow me. I saw them on my infrared trail camera memory card. I had positioned the cameras near the hallway. My lighting in the house would flicker whenever these orbs would show up. Something would also turn off my fan in the bedroom during these high orb activity periods. Orbs also were seen in my Alaska house and now in my condo in Illinois. These orbs mainly were white balls that flew all over the rooms. Very strange, indeed.

24

MY ANGELS LOOKING OVER ME

My sightings of the "Lady in White" happened twice in my life. From what I have heard, this phenomenon seems to have occurred to many people throughout history. My first sighting of the "Lady" was in 1972 while I was living with my parents after my military duty ended. My stay was temporary until I could find a place to stay. Around 1 AM, I woke up for a reason I could not figure out. I saw this tall lady dressed in a fluffy white gown that seemed to flow on the floor. She had a veil over her head, so her face could not be seen. This lady walked past my bed and went into my parents' bedroom. I followed her as she entered my parents' bedroom, but she disappeared as she approached my parents' bedside. She just faded away. I woke my mother up.

"Are you alright?" I asked her.

"Yes, I am OK. What is wrong?" She responded, groggily.

"I saw the "Lady in White" come into your bedroom."

"That is not unusual," She said, "I, too, have seen the 'Lady in White.'" My mother went on to say it might be Mother Mary from what she remembered from past sightings of people.

My Second Sighting of the "Lady in White"

In 1995, I saw the "Lady in White" in my Godfrey house in the bedroom around 2 AM. Again, I was awakened by something I could not figure out. Maybe the energy from the lady woke me up? The lady looked just as she did twenty years earlier at my parents' house. I saw her as she entered the bedroom door, so something prompted me to be awake and witness her visit. This time, I saw her face, and it was pure white as energy with a long flowing puffy gown with layers of material stretching to the floor. She walked past the foot of my bed and turned into the bathroom. I followed her but again, she slowly faded away. Is this an angel? I don't know, but she sure looked like an angel. My wife at the time saw nothing, and she was sound asleep. I felt good after witnessing these sightings of the lady. The lady must bring positive energy with her visitations.

My Angel was with me on this Day

On my usual annual trip to the southwestern States, I had an incident that I still think about to this day. I arrived in Gallup, New Mexico, on June 2, 2010, near the Hopi Reservation. I stayed at the El Rancho Hotel, where John Wayne stayed while making his iconic western movies. I stayed just one night because I was heading back south to visit friends in southern New Mexico. I went to the Zuni Indian Reservation twenty miles south of Gallup the following day. At around 9:30 AM, on June 3, 2010, on Highway 53, I arrived at Angel's Rock Butte. In front of the Butte was a gift shop, I stopped my car and thought I put the car in the parked gear while parking in the car parking lot. After securing my coffee and putting the car in park (I thought) I got out of my car. I got my camera out to take pictures of Angel's Rock and took a couple of photos, and the car started rolling.

When the car started rolling by itself, I was in disbelief because I am very organized regarding my car's status. The car turned on its own, heading down a slight decline or hill. I stopped filming and tried to jump in the vehicle to prevent the car from rolling down the small hillside. As soon as I leaped for the driver's seat, the car sped up, moving faster. After stumbling on the gravel, I tried to be a Hercules and hold the vehicle back. I fell face-first on the lot's gravel surface. I saw the left rear tire heading towards me, and I could not move in my position, being face down. The rear tire rolled over my right shoulder, but I did not feel the tire go over top of me. I could smelled the tire's rubber, so I knew I very was close to the tire. The car slowly moved down the embankment and across the two-lane highway as I watched the vehicle rolling.

When the car rolled over my right shoulder, I felt nothing hurting my shoulder, not even a pressure from the weight of my vehicle. A lady was yelling at me as she was coming out of an Indian roadside café.

"Are you alright?" She asked, worriedly.

"Yes, but my left leg was scraped very bad hanging on to the vehicle rolling."I answered.

"I saw the car wheel roll over your shoulder. Do you need an ambulance?"

I got up, and she looked at me, "The tire rolled over your right shoulder. You can see tire marks on your shirt."

"I'm okay, nothing hurts in my shoulder area. My left leg is hurting, though, it's all scratched up."

"You are lucky, the Angels were with you." She said.

"Well, there is Angel Rock right there on that butte." I pointed out. The gift shop people came over to me to check me out. The owner was a retired nurse and told me to come into the shop, so she could take care of my left leg. The husband said he would go to the car and bring it back up from the other side of the road. The car ended up running into a barbed-wire fence and had only a few tiny scratches. So, the car was lucky that day too. Unfortunately, I was wearing shorts, which made my leg scratches worse. When I fell and looked up at the car, I saw a Native American man looking at me from the café. He had said nothing to me. He just looked at me.

The guy that owned the gift shop recovered my car from the other side of the road. His wife, the retired nurse, cleaned up my left leg scratches in the shop. The shop owners said they see UFOs a lot where they are located and believe ETs are with us. The family of three was very nice to me and helped. The young son they had was also very helpful. They said the familiar phrase, "we were supposed to meet," a common theme I have been hearing from enlightened people. They showed me the shirt I was wearing, and they reiterated that the lady witnessing your accident saw your right shoulder run over by your car's tire. I kept the shirt and took pictures of it with the tire marks. There was something spiritual about this event with Angel Rock, the shop owners, and my Angels saving my shoulder from being crushed.

When I left the shop, I headed towards Roswell for my next stop. Then headed toward visiting my friends in Deming, New Mexico. When I got home, I spoke to my dealership's service manager, and he said the car sped up because the air conditioner kicked in, which speeds the car up for more rpm in order to run the air conditioner.

25

THE RECENT YEARS AND A VERY ACTIVE 2020 TO THE PRESENT

While in Alaska, I felt that there was less ET activity, especially the abduction type of events. I got many trail camera pictures that were fuzzy or just blanked out—I only got one decent picture that looks like a little grey ET. I told my wife visitations from ET had slowed down. Well, they must have heard me because the following incident happened to me the next night.

On July 14, 2014, I had another abduction event around 2 AM while in bed sleeping. I started feeling buzzing electrical energy coming up from both ankles up through my legs. They tingled and then went numb, and I could not feel my legs. The electrical power proceeded to my hands and arms, numbing them to where I could not move them. I felt a pencil-sized object in my right hand and a small nail clipper-sized thing in my left hand. I tried to throw both objects out of my hands, but I could not move due to being paralyzed.

My chest started to tingle, and my whole body went numb. It seems the paralyzing energy came up from my feet first and spread to my entire body. This was very typical of past paralyzing events by ET. After a short time, I cannot account for being paralyzed. It seemed I was finally able to throw the objects out of my hands because the paralyzing effect was starting to cease. Slowly, my hands got some motion back. At that point, my fear level increased, and I yelled out, "Help me, God." My wife said she heard me muttering something but could not figure out what I was saying. I was not fully asleep during this time of being paralyzed and I was somewhat conscious of the events. Unlike past abductions, there was no static electrical noise. I did not see any ETs near me or feel any presence. But, I knew something or someone was involved in what occurred to me, and the objects felt real.

Dark Humanoid Figures Next to My Bed

On December 27, 2017, in bed at 6 AM in Alton, Illinois, I had three dark human-looking figures standing next to me by my bed. This event took place in a half-awake status, I opened my eyes and saw the dark shadows of three beings. I could not see any faces or what clothing they had on, I could just barely make out dark shadowy silhouettes of humanoid beings. I was asleep as they were close to me in bed doing something to my body. When I woke up completely, they seemed to step back from me in bed.

When I woke up, I saw the shadows of these beings and punched my fist at them, knocking things off my nightstand. These dark figures turned and left slowly; one twisted my right foot down on the way out. It hurt when the foot was bent down from the big toe to the third toe. I could feel the fingertips of this being under my toes. A similar event took place in 2011 when the entity bent my right foot down. My wife woke up from the noise from the objects being knocked off the nightstand by my punch. After the foot bending, I said, "Oh God, they hurt my right foot again." My wife was partially awake after the noise of my punching, and she heard me saying, "Oh God" about my foot.

It seems that more than half of my experiences were done by the same ET species due to the repeated process they perform on my body. The bending of the foot tells me they make sure I am awake and well after their procedures on my body.

Injection in Right Shoulder of Blue Liquid

On February 23, 2019, in Alton, while sleeping in my bed, I experienced a very lucid dream that I feel was a regressed dream of an actual event. I dreamt that something or someone put a small canister about one inch wide with an injection needle at the end close to my right shoulder. The tube was filled with a blue liquid. I felt the stick of the needle, and then this entity injected the whole line of blue liquid into my arm. After that, I went unconscious and didn't remember anything.

I don't understand why the lucid dreams that I have regressed seem so real. It is often like watching a movie, and you are the main character. I am not a prolific writer or a creative artist, so these dreams come from my subconscious. Especially with the very topic of ETs, I have tangible contact within real-time. Regression works for me where hypnosis does not work.

The Year 2020 – Three months of ET Activity

Some of the scariest months in my house in Alton were from February to May 2020. It first started on February 6, 2020, at 12:30 AM. My dependable motion sensors were sounding out an alarm in the downstairs area. My wife had gone to the Philippines to visit her first grandson during this period. Next to my bed, I have a central alarm that gives off a high pitch sound when activated downstairs. There are two motion sensors on my back door and one on the front door. Of course, these sensors cover each room downstairs, giving comprehensive coverage and they have never failed to work correctly.

At 12:30 AM exactly, the alarms began going off. It was as though I had an intruder robber in the house. My adrenaline was up, and I hurriedly got my flashlight and weapon to check out the downstairs. I searched all over the downstairs and found nothing moving about. I checked the motion sensors and found them to be in good working order. Burglars compromised no doors or windows. I went back to bed a little nervous at this point. I kept my light and weapon close to me to ensure I would be ready if they tried to break in again. I had the distinct feeling that there was a presence in the house, you know that gut feeling that you are being watched. I trusted my alarms so deeply, I almost called the police. I decided to wait out any trouble. In less than two hours, the motion sensors alarm began to blare again. I was partially awake anyway, so I just listened for any sounds coming from downstairs while laying in bed.

After 2:30 AM, my motion sensors alarmed again, and of course, I was partially awake and listening intently for more sounds from downstairs. I felt ETs were visiting me by the way they were setting alarms off every two hours. The ETs were playing with me, letting me know they were in my house. I gave up on getting a good night's sleep and stayed alert most of the night. The motion sensors went off an additional five times from 12:30 AM to 8:30 AM. When my wife called just after 8 AM from the Philippines to let me know she was safely at our child's house, she heard the alarm go off.

"Your friends, the ETs are back, aren't they?" She asked.

"I think they're in the house." I responded, tiredly. They kept me up all night long. I checked out my downstairs and found that car lights nor ventilation were setting off the alarms. The sensors continued to work perfectly after that night.

Noises Upstairs

On February 8, 2020, I was downstairs watching TV when I heard a lot of racket, like boxes were being thrown around in our office room. I went upstairs to look at what had just happened and saw that a box of my wife's hairdressing articles and her hairdryer were strewn across the floor. This box was placed solidly on a shelf and should have never fallen over, especially with the neat way my wife puts things in order. The box was cleanly shoved off the shelf. This was the second mysterious incident in less than a week. The first was a pan in the kitchen that was dropped on the floor, making noise during daylight hours. My thoughts were that my ET visitors were invisible, so they were milling the house without being detected. I will find this invisibility to be a reality shortly.

I Placed an Infrared Trail Camera on my Kitchen Table

I made the decision to put one of my infrared trail cameras on my kitchen table because I felt entities were coming into my house in Alton. This was around February 6, 2020, and soon after the motion sensor alarms went crazy. On February 8, 2020, I set up the camera on the kitchen table. This is when I started picking up small and large orbs in the living room and kitchen. So, I knew if I waited long enough, I would catch an entity on my camera. When UFOlogists asked me why I put a motion-sensing infrared trail camera on my table inside the house, I said I was picking up a lot of motion from my alarms. I figured this was the best location to set up a camera. The orbs were several shapes, some were elongated shapes and others were distinct round spheres. It was like fishing. You must stay with patience to catch the big ones.

Shadow entity

The first strange picture I got was of a shadow person that showed up on my kitchen wall. It was just a long headed shadow ducking away from the camera lens. Around February 12, 2020, I captured the head shadow moving backward. I felt energized that I found something tangible to start my investigation with. I have the pictures on file of all these entities that my camera captured. I checked the location of the shadow head motion, and it did not correlate to the window or door in the kitchen. In other words, it was not a shadow produced by sunlight or cars. It was still daylight when these pictures were taken. My guess is that after all the videos and pictures that were taken, this shadow figure was part of the ET that showed up ten days later.

Michelin Man ET

On February 22, 2020, I got three consecutive pictures of an entity walking up my stairs to the second floor. This ET had a white bright space suit on that had concentric circles around the legs and midsection from what the camera caught. Of course, the infrared camera could have just seen a white glare from a heat return of the ET, making him white. The concentric circles are visible in the pictures. He had a slim elongated head that peered over the stairwell wall. There are no banisters or stair posts on my stairwell, so seeing something else is not the case. They could be mistaken for Michelin Man ET circles. The way he looked around the wall, this entity was very tall, around seven to eight feet tall. I tried the same steps, but nothing compares with his motion and height.

Reptilian ET

Several days later, on February 25, 2020, I got a huge surprise and felt fear when I looked at my camera memory card. I saw a motion at the top of the frame that looked to be an undulating jaw and forehead. It had stiff black hairs on what looked to be his cheek. The infrared diodes were blinking, causing the ET to open and close his eyes from the light. This ET looked directly into the camera lens, causing the video of fourteen seconds to be gritty and noisy. It was also dark, and I have tried to enhance the video to make out the ET better. People have a difficult time making out the video. The eyes on the bottom left of the frame opened and closed twice. I can make out the yellow color iris of its eyes and eyelashes like that of a human's eyes almost. It had dark green pitted skin like an alligator. The reptilian was very tall because he had to bend down to investigate the camera lens, he was maybe eight feet tall. The table was three and a half feet tall. The eyes scared me the most, it was as though they looked at me and sent a telepathic message. So, yes, it meant a lot to me seeing this video, even though some people don't see it.

Sent Pictures to MUFON and Writer

I sent the Michelin Man and the alligator-looking video to two of my friends, "Ed," a writer friend of mine, and "Joe" a Missouri MUFON Chief Field Investigator. They both got back to me several hours later, saying that the alligator-looking ET was a Reptilian in the fourteen-second video. They are both excellent researchers, so I trust and value their opinions. Joe told me that the white-suited ET picture going up my stairs was a Michelin Man ET. I got the name of this ET from Joe. He sent me an interview with a retired Air Force Colonel that he had done several years ago. Joe is also a film documentary expert. He passed this last year, and I miss him being involved in my UFO research. He was knowledgeable and friendly. When they both told me the other ET was a Reptilian, I got somewhat shook up about that finding. I saw a small one in my bedroom several years ago – the story is in this book. They look like giant cobras, and cobras are my worst nightmare. I knew nothing about the Michelin Man ET until Joe told me about them. This Air Force Colonel had told Joe they worked with the Michelin Man ETs in the Air Force and helped in technology.

This was the beginning of a three-month experience with these entities. I was glad my wife was away until April 2020 in the Philippines, as she would have been terrified of these visitors. My journey of keeping the camera rolling and taking EMF readings with the tri-field meter lasted three months while they came and went during that time. These were intense days of ET experiences. I have more coming up in this book about these three months.

Clapping Sounds when ET comes through Portals

When I heard a loud clapping sound, I knew it meant an ET or entity was coming into my house through a portal. It must be coming through a dimensional portal, and the clapping sound is made when they break through the barrier. If I am upstairs, I won't hear that clapping-like sound they make coming through dimensional walls.

My trail cameras don't have sound, so that won't be recorded. I sleep on the condo's second floor, so it would be hard to hear the clap from that distance. But I have heard to the clap when it was quiet.

One such entity, who I call the "Bright Entity", came through my back door in the kitchen area and materialized in the kitchen entrance area. My camera only picked up his entrance with streaming energy orbs and light streaks. He ended up standing at the kitchen door just out of camera reach. But I was able to get two seconds of his body in the doorway on a video camera. He came in through energy streams and materialized at the edge of the kitchen doorway. This was in March of 2020 when this entity appeared. Then after his materialization, orbs were set free in the kitchen area. These streams of light and spheres proved to me he came through a portal.

These three entities will be discussed later Reptilian, Michelin Man, and the light tall entity bright entity. These videos/pics were sent out to friends involved in UFO research. They both concurred that the films were of ET in nature. The orbs in all the rooms in the Condo were bright and solid enough to trigger my motion sensor camera to take pictures. I have many pictures of orbs on my memory sticks in the camera. My mother must have sensed ETs were visiting me after I told her of some of my activities in the Condo a couple of days ago. My mother called me the following day after my visitations and asked me if I was alright. Since my mother had numerous experiences with ET, she was concerned about my safety. Some family members think I will be taken someday and not returned. My family has also had experiences and knew the fear and possible abduction.

Three Months of ET Activity in My Condo

The three months I had ET interaction in February, March, April, and June 2020 was very intense, with something occurring almost daily. This all took place around March 8, 2020; my shampoo bottle was thrown into the bathtub while taking a shower. It was firmly on a large ledge of the tub area. The following day at around 5:30 AM, I heard a loud snapping sound, like fingers snapping, at least eight times. I listened to this snapping sound off to the left of my bed. At 6 AM, I heard a whistling sound like a human whistling for five seconds. Then I listened to a female's voice singing from out of nowhere after listening to a loud snap on the right side of the bed. They were letting me know they were with me in my house.

More Shadow Man Pictures

On March 9, 2020, I got more videos and pictures of a shadow man going up my stairs to my bedroom area. I have seen his shadow with my naked eyes in the condo moving around the house. This shadowy figure looks like a tall white or Palladian ET humanoid, maybe with his inviable cloaking on. The infrared camera picks up light and energy as just a bright light. The shadow man could be invisible; his shadow is cast on the walls and floor.

More MUFON Investigator findings

On March 9, 2020, MUFON Missouri Investigator "Joe" called me and said that he heard a mechanical sound on the cell phone recording taken off my computer screen. I had filmed the reptilian video coming off my desktop computer because of a significant file download problem with my desktop computer. It ultimately was quicker to record off my computer screen with a cell phone until I got a site for large files. Joe said he heard chattering like a metallic sound coming from recording. The trail camera also does not have audio capabilities. It seems my cell phone picked up the sound over my shoulder while I was filming the computer screen. Joe said it did not sound like a human chattering. I sent the sound video to my friend Ed, and he forwarded the video to a sound expert. The sound expert wrote Ed back and said it was not human and sounded like a metallic chattering. He said it was like some type of communication and was not a hoax. The sound expert could not document it officially due to his job reputation but he helped me figure out the chattering sound anyway and let me know the reptilian I was filming off the computer screen produced the sound. So, the reptilian was looking over my shoulder, watching me film the computer screen image of him. I did not hear his chatter because it was a magnetic metallic sound only the cell phone could record. Another fact is that these ETs are invisible walking around us.

Magnetic Readings with Tri-Field Meter in Condo

On March 14, 2020, I was in my office room at the condo and felt the presence of an entity. I got out my K2 meter and my tri-field meter and took measurements of the room. This was after I got another alarm downstairs with my motion sensors. I took these readings at 3 AM and 10 AM. I made sure to take magnetic readings in the living room and kitchen. They were both low readings with ambient readings below 1mg. The EMF readings were high outside my bedroom area in the hallway and the top of the stairs, reading 3.5mg and clipping out at that EMF range. Nothing of any power source was in these two areas. It seems the ET entities are transported to the bottom of my stairs then move around. The office area usually had 3.5mg clipped out readings of EMF in areas where electrical power cannot corrupt the actual tasks. My K2 meter reads the highest light (red) in the office and top of the stairs. Both testers are used to verify readings. This tells me the ETs whereabouts in the Condo. I showed these readings to Ed via a cell phone recording taken in the office area. My brother Dan witnessed the high readings, being careful to avoid ambient readings. He saw the tri-field meter clipping out over 3.5mg. I figured the ETs were peaceful and just observing my work on Radio and pictures. I felt they meant no harm, so I felt safe with them. I had three ETs visit me around the same time. I have a video and pictures of the three: the Michelin Man, the Reptilian, and the tall bright glowing ET or Palladian.

I felt a buzzing sensation in my stomach during high-energy readings around 6 AM on March 21, 2020. I was in bed trying to sleep. I felt like an energy-twisting feeling on my last rib for several seconds.

I had felt these energy buzzing feelings before but not this strong. ETs use electrical, magnetic energy to immobilize a person to do what they want to do peacefully. Is this wrong? Yes, any intrusion into our bodies is terrible without permission. With the condo's high energy, I expected to get energy directed at me for purposes I am not sure about.

Orbs and EMF Energy Remains in Condo

My wife returned home from the Philippines in late April, and it seemed to slow the ET action down. It still had high readings of EMF energy, so something was still in the Condo. Some of the last motion sensor alarms went off on May 5, 2020, and orbs remained in the house but not as many. The office room still had a lot of energy, and the wife preferred not to work at her desk for her fear of the ETs and energy. There was still 3.5mg of EMF higher in the office area, excluding the ambient readings. My thought was that the condo was part of a portal they traveled through. Either to visit me and possibly others. The orbs seem to stay around the longest because I think they are drones for ETs to spy on us.

The ETs Were Still in the Condo

On May 16, 2020, I moved my trail camera to the foot of the stairs to make sure the ETs were gone. It seems there was one last ET that showed up at the condo. When I checked my camera's thumb card for pictures, I first found a lot of orbs again. Then something mysterious showed up on the far right of the video frame. This tall, very bright white light materialized from long strings of energy coming from the kitchen door on the far-right side. After total materialization, this brilliant white entity looked eight feet tall standing in the kitchen hallway. His head was the last thing to bounce into shape, and it reared back very fast. This white entity is only seen for three seconds on the video. But the energy was still coming from him as long streaks of light and round orbs. These orbs went all over the kitchen area, varying in size and light density. This video proved that these entities were transported from another dimension or a UFO overhead. His head seemed to be wrapped in cloth like a mummy when you still frame the video. This all happened in a matter of three seconds, his materializing. No doubt, after materializing, he went invisible to walk around us in the condo. Lucky to have the infrared camera that picks up light sources. I have the video of this entity.

Paranormal and High Energy Readings

For the latest weird events of 2021, I put the trail camera in the office area of the condo targeting a table desk. May 30, 2021, the camera picked up some movement from the top of the table. Something white and black quickly pushed a couple of books about two inches across the table. It happened within two seconds. Luckily, the camera picked up the motion even though it was quick. Another motion triggered the trail camera motion sensor before this part of the video camera filmed this action due to the short timing of the two-second filming. Interesting because one of the two books shoved a couple of inches was the Bible. Maybe some dimensional entity was directing me to the Bible to read a passage. Messages from ETs or dimensional sources are always given in code or movement.

Constant High EMF Readings

I took regular EMF readings with my tri-field meter in our condo ever since the ETs visited the year before. During their visit in 2020, I got over 3.5mg, where there shouldn't have been little or no EMF. I regularly read EMF energy from March 18, 2021, to May 2021. I would check for all ambient readings first, like wall outlets, lamps, where the power panel was located regarding readings and electrical wires in the walls. These had to be ruled out before accurate EMF readings could be ascertained. My meter pegged out on the 3.5mg scale on my body and head areas. It also pegged out over 3.5mg where I was sitting. During the ET visits, I got 20mg on the hundred scales in certain rooms at varying times. In our living room, there is a regular 3.5mg plus reading. It was always 20mg plus on the one hundred scales in our living room in Alaska. It was uncomfortable to sit and watch TV in that room. Our condo still has 3.5mg in most areas, excluding ambient points. I understand that 1.5mg and over regularly is not healthy for humans. So, what are our electronics and cell phones doing to us?

Swirling Energy in my Body During Sleep

On May 2, 2021, while in bed in Alton around 5:30 AM, I had circular swirling energy occurring from my chest to my waistline. Some of the power went into my arms, and it felt like a tingling sensation.As I said earlier it was an electrical, magnetic energy that is causing this feeling. This has happened to me several times in all my experiences. Some energies are more powerful, and some are softer and gentler. Gentler, maybe because it is healing energy. It gives me more of a spiritual feeling when it is a milder tingling sensation.

Usually, I sleep on my right side on account of my back. This night I was sleeping on my back, and I didn't start sleeping that night. I felt somebody put me on my back for some reason. This felt like an abduction because of my body position, and the electrical energy dissipated from my body after ET brought me back to my bed. I did not hear intense crackling sounds around me or remember much about what happened. I would rather choose to think it was spiritual healing instead of an abduction. I have had too many electrified abductions and would like some spiritual healing.

Small unknown Instrument Directed Energy at My Face

A recent strange event happened on December 8, 2021, sometime after 3 AM again, while I was in bed. I woke up out of sleep and sat on my bed because I heard a noise. I felt like something was moving around my bed. I saw a small device about ten inches wide with gray grid-like vertical fins in the front of the device that was eight inches long and one inch wide. This grid was in front of the device, and its body was ten inches wide and twelve inches long from what I saw of it. The color of the main body of the device was white. I thought it was an ET drone spying on us at the very first second of seeing this device. I could not see behind the machine or who was using this device. My afterthought was that this device was intelligently operated.

Without much time to think, this device shot out a loud buzzing vibrating sound. There was also a static electrical charge that was popping and snapping. Almost felt like I could see the waves of energy hitting my face and head. I have never seen or heard such noises all combined. Extraordinary experience being hit in the face with this device.

My head felt the magnetic pulling of my face and energy surging through my head. I experienced my body surging and vibrating with energy. My eyes were out of focus, and I had to close them to stop the pain that was occuring. My ears began popping, and I felt like I was underwater, and they hurt like a loud noise penetrating the ears. This lasted about five seconds, and I had no time to figure out what had happened. I got the device's description the first second or two before being shot with energy. After that, I passed out on the bed but quickly woke up a few minutes later. My wife, again, did not hear anything during this encounter. I was even afraid to tell her about this event because it would scare her, having ETs in her bedroom. I am glad she does not want to hear about my research. She saw my drawing on my computer desk that I drew of this device.

"What is that?" She asked.

"Just a picture of something I saw years ago." I said, brushing it off.

"Don't tell me, you know I am afraid of this evil stuff."

"It is not bad. It is just life outside of our world," I responded.

This event with the strange device would not be included in this book, but this happened with all the bodily effects and pain I experienced. Being shot with energy by this device could have been a lucid, regressed dream, but I felt it happened in the present. My thoughts are, was this a consciousness download from ET or an energy attack that might harm my health? One of my mystery scientists said it screened my mind and consciousness. The device takes readings of my mind and stores information. I don't know the answer, just theories.

Evidence of Movement Near my Bedside

As I have said throughout this book, I have ET experiences even to this day. A lifetime of events, I keep wondering, "*what do they want?*" On December 10, 2021, at 9 AM, when I woke up from bed, I could not find my cell phone. I keep it on my nightstand next to me, a couple of feet away. I saw it on the floor halfway down the bed, in the middle of the bed. It never falls that far away from the nightstand when I drop it by accident. The flashlight on the cell phone was on and pointed towards the ceiling, which is how I found it. The charging cable was off, and it is always on charging while I sleep. It was like somebody pulled it off the charger and tossed it with the flashlight on. I usually have a hard time turning on the flashlight.

On December 15, 2021, I got up around 9 AM, just like I usually do. My cell phone was missing again. I had hooked it up to a charging cable as usual. This time I found my cell phone halfway under my bed, about five feet away from the nightstand where it sits and charges. My reading glasses and a table ornament were also on the floor. It seems somebody just swiped their arm at the nightstand and knocked it all off. With the cell phone being on the charging cable, how does it get tossed five feet and halfway under my bed? I did mention in the book that I had shadows near me, and I punched at them. I knocked my cell phone off the nightstand, but it fell close to the nightstand. My wife woke up during this commotion. So, why didn't she hear this commotion of the cell phone being tossed?

Abduction Types

I mentioned earlier that I woke up at 3 AM and had a freezing body on September 2, 2021, the fifth freezing body event in five years. I spoke to a couple of very reliable scientists in UFO research. They mentioned that it could have been a quantum leap or a jump in the waveform. I was riding the wave, as one researcher put it. More scientific is what they called a singularity through collapse wave-particle. Meaning the ETs took your energy, soul, mind, and consciousness to another dimension leaving your physical body behind. It would be like an Avatar or hologram matrix. One of the methods of abductions I mentioned earlier was a bedside abduction. I asked them what would happen if they did not put my energy, soul, mind, and consciousness back in time. Would I die? I felt dead, waking up frozen during these freezing events. Which abduction type would you choose if ET let you have a choice? Whole-body abduction? Bedside body in place with DNA and semen or eggs are taken? Or quantum leap abduction with your soul, energy, mind, and consciousness took in a hologram?

CONCLUSION

MY OBSERVATION OF WHAT ARE UFOS / UAPS

When this author was younger, I would look up at the stars and wonder if people were in the vast universe looking at us. Little did I know I would find out throughout my life the answers. They were coming to our planet to visit and live here on their bases on earth. The big kid question back when I was a child was, *"Where is the end to the Universe?"* Of course, the answer is infinity. Do we know what infinity means? We had a big scare back in the 1950s to avoid flying saucers and run if you see them. Yes, I am older now and can formulate a better-informed answer. My experiences have taught me what I need to know. UFOs/UAPs do exist, and this Author is one hundred percent sure they are real. I have seen six close-up UFOs, numerous orbs, and far-away sightings. When you see your first up-close UFO, you become an automatic believer and have a lifelong hunger to know more about what you witnessed. Our governments and militaries have denied UFOs existence all around the world. People like me and others who have had UFO experiences wonder why they don't tell the truth? Our government is starting to disclose that UFOs and UAPs exist. That gives us crazy UFO buffs a reason to say, "we told you so." My whole family has seen UFOs, and many more people worldwide are seeing more UFOs than ever.

What are UFOs/UAPs? Some of the ET spacecraft are stationed right here on earth in underground facilities. There's supposedly a moon base with UFOs stationed in the moon itself, and NASA knows this but keeps it secret. Other UFO ET craft is also stationed on Mars, which is a secret. As some proposed, the ETs spacecraft are anti-gravity spacecraft fueled by element 115 and mercury. We don't know exactly how they are made, but they defy gravity and move faster than we can comprehend. I had a lucid dream of seeing element 119, and it looks like granules of silver- and charcoal-colored small pellets. Scientists say that element 119 would look like if we could produce it. I usually research what I see in lucid dreams, which I saw. They say we have a lot of work yet to develop element 119.

A UFO craft is a self-contained gravity enclosure to protect occupants from high G forces. A shield of gravity protection surrounds the whole UFO craft, which is why the occupants can withstand the unimaginable speed and turn maneuvers. Scientists and Ufologists say that the UFO craft pulls space towards craft, propelling them. Anti-gravity forces surround the craft, and when that happens, it takes very little propulsion to push it forward, almost like our space solar-powered kites pulling itself across space. Do I know for sure what I just wrote is true? These are all theories that scientists have proposed, and I am repeating these theories. Element 119 is the only part of these theories that I have seen and suggested. There are many different UFOs/UAPs, and I imagine it varies with each ET race. I saw six of them, so I know what they look like. All six of these crafts are listed and pictured in this book. There are wormholes that the ETs travel with their craft through to get to other dimensions and universes. Their anti-gravity forces can travel these wormholes. Our scientists are still researching wormhole possibilities of travel and time travel through wormholes. My family and I have seen bright orbs dropping through our atmosphere from a single area of the sky. They would drop down and blink twice and leave very rapidly. We have repeatedly witnessed portals dropping orbs out that are UFOs from the sky.

Extraterrestrial and Dimensional Beings

Starting at the age of thirteen years, I have been blessed at seeing UFOs - otherworldly craft. Often thought who are in those crafts and flying them. I was in several onboard craft and witnessed the inside of the UFOs. These observations come to me through lucid regressed dreams in a deep sleep. This was after a physical sighting of a UFO. I believe that regressed dreams are more credible when a tangible sighting of a UFO occurs. The first one I was on was dark and warm, and I could not see the ETs but knew they were there. ET usually erases memories, and sometimes you can regress parts of the event if they leave them in your subconscious. When I see the ETs, I never see their faces except for a couple that allowed me to see them. Regressed dreams showed me a tall woman that was pale white with no hair. She looked me right in the face, and I walked to a panel with her on the ship. Then she led me to a transport tunnel or hallway to come back home. These experiences are written in this book. I am just building up to one plain fact: that ETs exist and have been here on earth for thousands of years.

Another regressed dream showed me a small four-foot-tall baby-faced human-looking ET with bright blue eyes. Their skin was pale white but looked very human, and they were wearing white space suits with yellow helmets. They were preparing to be transported to another location. They wanted me to see that operation on a supply craft for some reason. I also saw a blue hybrid ET that seemed to be almost human. His arms were spotted with blue spots and recognizable as a blue hybrid entity. The ETs let me see the arms for some reason, and the arms had tiny fine hairs on them. They were showing me that they are close to us humans in appearance. I can include this regressed dream along with the others mentioned here. I had a regressed dream that I was on a dark ship, and a tall white lady greeted me, but the other male, ET said he would lead me. In these regressed dreams, none of the ETs spoke to me. They communicated telepathically in which I was able to understand what they wanted me to do. I was led to a dark room where a large reptilian ET lay back in a large, curved seat or pilot chair. The ET that led me to that room, I could only see his body, not his face. He had on a gray suit and was very tall, so he must have been a tall white ET. I stood there looking at this reptilian in the oversized chair while this tall white ET kissed this reptilian on the forehead. Then the tall white male left the room. I surmised that the tall whites were workers for the reptilians. Have they maybe captured enemies? I explain the reptilian appearance in this book.

The following three meetings of ETs were in person, no regressed dream. These events proved to me that these other regressed ETs were very real. The first I met in 1995, and he was a three-and-a-half-foot tall grey ET. He walked up to the side of my bed, looking right in the face. I was shocked for a few seconds but passed out from his energy. I am sure he was doing a bedside DNA and semen sampling. He was very wrinkled and ugly, but he had no dark covers over his eyes. The second in-person meeting was with "Hiroko" in Sedona, and I spent a whole day with her – she was strange. The proof she was ET was that she came to my house with the two younger sons. May I call them my sons? They dumbed my cousin and me down, and we could not talk, making it a further fact they were ET. So, I saw three ETs that day in person. The third accurate in-person contact was with a five-and-a-half-foot tall young reptilian standing and staring at me when I got up out of bed. He stood near my closet for only five seconds, but this scared me more than any ET contact. I am afraid of cobras, and this thing looked like a cobra.

CONCLUSION 2

Do I believe ETs exist? Without a doubt, I think seeing is believing. ETs have been on our earth for not thousands but millions of years. History has it wrong about our human existence. ETs manipulated our DNA for thousands of years.

Dimensional Beings

Dimensional beings come from another dimension other than our dimension. The confusion about ETs and dimensional beings is whether they can escape their dimension? I say, yes, they can. Dimensional beings come through the thin veil between our dimension and theirs. They can walk in our thinly veiled 3rd dimension from a possible seven dimensions the Koran and Judea principles mention. We don't know about more dimensions, but seven dimensions are mind-boggling. I have videos of these dimensional beings coming into my house. They are bright white glowing entities that are transported from dimension to dimension. It seems they are brought into our dimension by a long rope looking light. A couple of white cord rope-looking energy beams bring them into our existence. After their complete materialization, numerous orbs bounce all over the room. They can use an invisibility cloak to walk beside us in our own houses. I caught several light beings on video with infrared camera capabilities. You can't see them with your naked eye. Infrared picks up heat and energy on film. Final note – Sasquatch is possibly a dimensional being.

On the other hand, the ETS can be beamed down from a UFO craft to your location. They can be invisible and walk-through walls. A Reptilian and a Michelin Man ET have also been in my house, and I have a film of both. My infrared camera picks them up on video, but I cannot see them with my eyes. This house intrusion by the ETs happened in 2020, and the stories are in this book. I think they were beamed down from a ship and inspected my property without me seeing them, they were invisible, and my camera picked up their images on video, and they knew about the camera being on. Reptilian looked closely into the camera and blurred the video. The Michelin Man turned and looked at the camera on his way up the stairs. The camera picked up on bright flashes, so that is when the ETs beamed into my house. ETs can be transported by wormholes, as mentioned before, in their ships. It is not clear if they make quantum leaps in dimensions the same way dimensional beings do in this author's experience. I can only say what I saw.

Abductions

Abductions are challenging to figure out; unlike seeing a UFO or ET, it is intangible. I have difficulty coming to terms with ETs and their purpose for invading our bodies without our permission. My brother asked me how many times I had been abducted. I said I could count about six times in my life that they either left an implant or almost electrocuted my body. Considering the years' ET has tracked me, my actual figure of abduction will be much more than six times. Most of the time, you are knocked out and don't realize you were examined, and DNA extraction was performed. Again, fifty percent of people don't know they have been abducted sometime in their lives. Most of my abductions were not painful, nor was I hurt during the abduction.

There were exceptions of three abductions that I was almost electrocuted during the abduction process. I was under an anesthetic feeling with other abductions feeling like I was on a cloud, so I did not know anything.

From my experiences, I have learned that ETs perform abductions to know about our bodies and how well we are with our polluted environment. These are my theories based on my experience and knowledge tracked by ETs all my life. There are several possibilities why ETs examine us and take DNA and semen/eggs. They use our biological materials to fertilize hybrids to change our human race into a more intelligent, peaceful race of humans. Not only do they take biological samples from humans, but they also take samples of DNA from animals – animal mutilations. There are other human-populated planets out in our wondrous universe, and they could be taking animal DNA to help feed humans or hybrids. They are also using frequency testing equipment to measure our DNA frequencies. Each person has their frequency, and ETs use this test to see how well we are health-wise. ETs also know if they are interested in using a person's DNA to hybridize their population. The most compelling reason for abducting humans is to see if they can improve an abductee's DNA to make them more intelligent and peaceful. This is not a bad idea to improve upon a human being. There has been genius' that surprisingly just popped up from nowhere in our history. Young kids today are getting more talented and more intelligent than at any time in our human history. The worse scenario is that they are making people into hybrids on earth and in space on large Noah Arc ships to take over our planet.

My experience has brought me to this conclusion; there are three types of abductions. They may all have similar reasons for taking humans and examining them for DNA purposes. Each abduction has its fears and the feeling of helplessness. The third way of abducting that I will explain is a new form of abduction I just noticed this past two years.

1. An actual physical abduction is where they take your body

to a ship or to another location or dimension to do their exams and collect DNA, blood, and memory readings of your consciousness. Then you are returned most of the time to the same place they picked you up. Sometimes you are several miles from your last location, and you have missing time.

2. Bedside abduction is where the ETs do all their work on you while you are in bed. The person next to you is dumbed down with magnetic energy, and they know nothing of what is going on. I was involved in these abductions many times with semen and DNA sampling. The ETs also use frequency detectors to read your subconscious mind and the health of your DNA. If you wake up during the ETs testing, you will probably remember pieces of the event, like kicking the small hose from your groin while they are taking semen. It also depends on how much the ETs want to let you remember to ponder their superiority over you.
3. The freezing of your body so ETs can take your energy, soul, and mind consciousness. They leave your body and bring these elements with them and put your essence in a hologram or matrix. They take your holographic body to another dimension or planet like an Avatar type of transfer. They can examine your consciousness and teach you the knowledge and plant it deep in your subconscious to use at a time of their choosing. How do you know this happens? You feel frozen like you are dead, wake up in a panic, and shake terribly from being frozen. When they restore your energy, soul, and mind-consciousness, you are so exhausted you go back to sleep very quickly, only remembering your frozen body. This has happened to me six years in a row, on or about the same date, telling me I get an annual follow-up from ET. A brilliant scientific mind said that they call a quantum leap or jumping the waveform. In other big words, it is called singularity

> through a collapse wave-particle. A black box followed my right foot in the regressed dream with a tall, white ET woman. Could this box be carrying my soul for protection?

In most abductions, you might end up with strange unknown scars. Maybe even an implant you may or may not notice for a long time. Most scars are holes in the skin in numbers of three in a row or two. These holes are sometimes linked with scratches to the skin. There have been triangle scars, circular scars, and bruises where they handled your body. I have had two implants that I have found because the insertion points were still red, like a small red needle hole or a thin red laser line. I have had many scratches to my left leg that I could never figure out. I don't do hard work or hike in the wilderness, so where do I get these scars? I still have two implants in my left thumb and right shoulder. Most implants are placed on the left side of the body. The ET no doubt uses the heart as a reference to implant your body mainly on the left side. The holes in the skin could take deeper DNA samples or inject you with tagging fluid to manipulate your DNA. Implants come in two forms. The biological form is made from carbon elements and their DNA controlling properties that cling to our DNA. The metal implants might work mainly on the nervous system to make frequent changes to your body. They could also be radio transmitting implants that send messages to the ETs for tracking or detecting body changes.

Apports

Apports are another mystery that appears out of nowhere. These are coins, feathers, trinkets, ornaments, and most jewelry are given to you to get your attention. These Apports could come from another entity in a dimension or a passed loved one in that dimension. I have learned about Apports when you find one; it is your first thought from the heart who gave this to you. ET is possible if you think it gives you Apports to let you know they are tracking you. I believe that

ETs are watching me and letting me know they are still with me. Apports have been given to me from Illinois to Alaska, so good tracking of my frequencies by the ETs. When you find white feathers, it is from a loved one that just passed. That has happened to me several times. My most bizarre Apports were little round plastic disc I found on the floor in front of me or my pockets. I found two plastic discs in Illinois and found two discs in Alaska – hard to explain.

Consciousness

Been learning how critical consciousness is when you understand ETs and the universe. Consciousness is being taught in the military and other agencies. Having consciousness is knowing yourself and your fate. To understand consciousness, you must know your place in the universe and have the knowledge and respect for all life—acceptance of yourself and being confident in what you know. The higher your consciousness, the higher dimensions you might travel in the afterlife. The Native American Indians understand nature and the higher realms. NASA uses Native American Indians to train astronauts to accept the unusual and culturally different races of people or ETs. This is training for astronauts landing on Mars. Teaching astronauts to try to comprehend the things they don't understand. The ETs wait for all humans to raise their consciousness and be a more peaceful civilization. Then maybe they will disclose themselves to us and talk to us. Our government's UFO disclosure will keep coming out slowly in drips and drops. Will, we ever get complete disclosure information from our governments - probably not.

ABOUT THE AUTHOR

My birthplace was in Illinois, the great Midwest at the beginning of the 1950s. A time when kids played outside in the dirt and a cardboard box was the best toy. We did not have computers, but we always had neighborhood kids to play with. My mother told me to mention I was born with gray, long pretty sideburns at birth. So, my mystery might have started on my first day of life. My mother had her ET/UFO experiences when she was younger and still has strange things happen to her today – she is 94 years old now. I blame her for giving all eleven brothers and sisters the UFO enlightenment from her DNA. The family considers this open-mindedness a blessing.

I graduated from High School with honor roll grades, so the computers never helped me. Learned the old school way of reading books and writing until our hands got tired. Having a large family and a father that worked a blue-collar job, we had to be creative to make a few dollars as kids. My older brother and I played music while going to school, and it helped pay our school fees. Music was also a blessing to our family because seven brothers ended up playing and singing music (The Crystal Image Band). I had to start working at a Steel Mill after my graduation ceremony. No graduation party for me because of the early wake-up time for work.

My older brother and I enlisted in the Army after High School on the buddy plan because the draft was after us. I went into Nuclear Weapons training, and my brother went into communications electronics. I got a top-secret security clearance but did not like the constant oversight of military intelligence. Being a 19-year-old teenager, I did not like the restrictive life of a top-secret soldier. I went to the post chaplain to get out of class with an eighty-nine percent average in the school. I got out of that class, but I was a free agent from my military contract. So, I ended up in Vietnam as a combat platoon sergeant. After one year in combat, I decided to take my honorable discharge after three years of service plus turning down an officer's commission.

After service, I worked a blue-collar job and went to night school. I was still playing music, working, and attending College. Graduated from a Junior College and a Radio & TV broadcasting school in St. Louis, Missouri. After that, I went to Lindenwood College, majoring in mass communications in St. Charles, Missouri. I worked in a couple of Radio Stations, but I wanted to earn more, so I took a job in Chicago in X-ray equipment sales. My occupations were: Electrician, Red Cross Disaster Manager, Refinery Lead Man, small business manager, and I owned my Restaurant Nightclub for a short time. Yes, I played music all these years while working full-time.

Today, I am a Radio/video Host on DNN – Disclosure News Network. Being retired, I try to keep busy. That is why I decided to write this book about my lifelong UFO/ET experiences. My experiences started at thirteen years of age. Since then, I have had a hunger to get the truth out to the public. Try to cut through all the disinformation and lies by the ruling class. My experiences continue to this day, and it seems every event teaches me more about our Universe and other life forms – Extraterrestrials & Dimensional Entities. I hope you enjoy this book "They," what do they want? I mainly want people to see similarities in their experiences with this book. Hopefully, I can help you find answers to ET experiences and abductions.

AFTERWORD

Go to HangarıPublishing.com to learn more about the Author and stay up to date with their newest releases.

BOOK DEDICATIONS

I wish to thank the following people in my life that supported my efforts to write this book. Everybody needs a support system to get things done, and I got Blessed with these great people.

My wife has supported my research and wanted me to write this book for the past few years. Even though she did not wish to deal with my study of this topic of ETs directly, she supported my beliefs. Before marriage, she did not know anything about UFOs, but through osmosis, with my experiences, she believes me now. She has witnessed some strange things around me and our house, which led to her support. I want to thank her for her help and love.

My mother, Stella Emmons, is a huge supporter of this book. She often checks my progress on how the book is coming along. My mother is 94 years old and still mentally sharp. She has had many strange ET and UFO experiences herself; she is why all our family has UFO experiences through her DNA frequencies. I must also mention the twenty-five percent of Crowe American Native Indian blood in her body. Both have been factors in family tracking by ET as proposed by Ufologist. I want to thank my mother for her support and love.

I want to thank the two people instrumentally involved in helping me with my book's preliminary work. Doug Hajicek, Publisher, and Alex Hajicek, Publisher, at Hangar 1 Publishing. Very nice people with a reputable history of publishing books. I am very fortunate to meet these two knowledgeable men. Thank you, Doug & Alex.
https://hangar1publishing.com/

Olof Rocker, from Sweden, helped me with twelve drawings in the book. His artistic talents are superior and detailed. I want to thank him for his talented artwork. He came along when I needed him the most.
https://www.instagram.com/olof_rockner/

Made in United States
North Haven, CT
13 February 2023

32556360R10104